"If you have knowledge, let others light their candles at it"

Margaret Fuller

FASCINATING STORIES AND FACTS

A COLLECTION OF INTERESTING STORIES FROM HISTORY, SCIENCE & CULTURE

Billy Brainiac

FactBrainiac.com

Fact Brainiac Publishing

TABLE OF CONTENTS

THE BOOK THAT PREDICTED TITANIC'S DEMISE

In 1898, American writer Morgan Robertson published a novella called Futility, which told the story of a massive British ocean liner called the Titan. The fictional vessel was considered unsinkable—until it struck an iceberg and sank in the North Atlantic, killing most of its 3,000 passengers due to a lack of lifeboats.

The premise sounds eerily familiar, right? That's because 14 years later, the events of Robertson's book played out in real life. The "unsinkable" RMS Titanic met a tragic fate under extremely similar circumstances, making Robertson seem clairvoyant.

But Was It Really Clairvoyance?

After the Titanic disaster of 1912, people credited Robertson with somehow predicting the future. But Robertson himself denied any psychic powers. He was simply knowledgeable about the shipbuilding industry and maritime trends.

Futility by Morgan Robertson

By following technological advances in ship design, Robertson realized that massive ocean liners were the way of the future. He deduced that the race for building bigger and faster ships could lead to hubris about their indestructibility. This gave him the idea for Futility.

Robertson's Extensive Seafaring Experience

What allowed Robertson to so accurately envision the Titanic catastrophe was his hands-on experience working at sea. He spent a full decade aboard various American merchant vessels, getting first-hand knowledge of how ships operated. He saw how the maritime industry was evolving in the late 19th century toward larger luxury liners.

After leaving life at sea, Robertson pursued writing fiction. He authored several titles about maritime adventures, underscoring his ongoing interest in ships and seafaring culture. This lent authenticity to the nautical details in Futility.

Uncanny Similarities Between Fact and Fiction

Robertson's fictional Titan was the largest ship of its day, touted as unsinkable, and carried far too few lifeboats for its 3,000 passengers. In April 1912, the real RMS Titanic set sail with nearly identical specifications and weaknesses.

Below is a comparison of some key attributes of the Titan and Titanic:

- Length: 800 ft (Titan), 882 ft (Titanic)
- Top Speed: 25 knots (Titan), 22.5 knots (Titanic)
- Lifeboat Capacity: 500 people (Titan), 1,178 people (Titanic)
- Passengers: 3,000 (Titan), 2,224 (Titanic)
- Month of Sinking: April (both)
- Time of Sinking: Around Midnight (both)
- Cause of Sinking: Collision with iceberg on Starboard side (both)
- Survivors: 13 (Titan), 705 (Titanic)

Morgan Robertson, author of Futility

Beyond these similarities, the Titan also sank on a starry night after hitting the iceberg along its starboard side. Futility even featured a shipboard conspiracy and cover-up around the collision, just like some Titanic conspiracy theories.

Success After a Disaster

When news broke of the real Titanic tragedy, Robertson republished his book as The Wreck of the Titan, capitalizing on the notoriety. The reprint outsold the original release.

While profiting from a disaster may seem distasteful, Robertson's literary prescience was remarkable. He possessed an uncanny ability to imagine how the quest for lavish ships could end in catastrophe. Or was it just a lucky guess? We'll never know for sure.

Robertson's life after writing Futility remained somewhat mysterious. He died in 1915, just three years after the Titanic sank. One can only imagine how eerie he must have found the parallels between his fiction and the real-life events that stunned the world. But he took advantage of the serendipity by reissuing his previously overlooked book for a new audience.

While Robertson denied being a fortune teller, his insights did prove prophetic. He will be remembered for one of literature's strangest predictions—even if it was simply a case of art imitating life before life had a chance to imitate art.

LEONARD DA VINCI'S HORSE

In the heart of the bustling city of Milan, a grand sculpture known as "Leonardo's Horse" stands majestically, a testament to both the genius of the Renaissance artist Leonardo da Vinci and the dedication of a modern-day art lover from Pennsylvania.

The Commission from the Duke

the late 15th century, Leonardo was already a recognized figure in the field of art and engineering. His reputation caught the eye of Ludovico Sforza, the Duke of Milan, who commissioned Leonardo to create the grandest equestrian statue the world had ever seen. This monument was to honor Ludovico's father, Francesco, marking a significant chapter in Leonardo's artistic journey.

Leonardo's design of the horse

Leonardo embraced the challenge with his characteristic fervor and began planning a 24-foot tall clay model. This was to serve as the blueprint for the final statue, intended to be cast in bronze.

As he meticulously worked on this project, Leonardo also fulfilled other commissions, producing masterpieces such as "The Last Supper."

Chaos Ensues

However, the world of politics can be as chaotic as it is relentless. The Duke of Milan, in an attempt to fortify his defenses against Venice, allowed French troops to pass through his territory. But in a sudden turn of events, the French troops turned against the Duke. The bronze set aside for Leonardo's horse was urgently converted into weapons, shifting the focus from art to survival

Mould design to cast Leonardo's Horse

In 1499, the French forces seized Milan, marking the end of a golden age. The magnificent clay model of the horse was reduced to rubble by French archers using it for target practice.

The Mourning Artist

It seemed like Leonardo's ambitious project had met an untimely end. His sketches and molds disappeared in the chaos, and the grand horse became a beautiful dream that never came to fruition. Legend suggests that Leonardo mourned having never completed this ambitious project.

There is a story from the early 1500s, where during a conversation about Dante's Divine Comedy in a Florence piazza, a stumped Leonardo da Vinci suggested they ask the incoming Michelangelo for insight. However, Michelangelo, mistaking Leonardo's genuine query for mockery, scornfully retorted, "Explain it yourself."

Adding insult to injury, he jeered "You, who designed a giant horse to cast in bronze and failed. And then abandoned it out of shame." The encounter concluded abruptly, leaving a red-faced Leonardo in its wake.

Lost and Found

Fast forward five centuries to 1965, Leonardo's lost notebooks were discovered in Madrid. These books, now known as the Codex Madrid II, included sketches for the elusive horse. This intriguing revelation caught the attention of Charles C. Dent, a retired airline pilot and art collector from Pennsylvania. Dent read about Leonardo's horse in a 1977 National Geographic magazine. Dent was moved by the story of Leonardo's unrealized dream and decided to pick up where the Renaissance master left off.

Horse study by Leonardo Da Vinci

Homage to Leonardo

Bringing aboard the talented sculptor Nina Akamu, Dent embarked on an artistic journey to breathe life into Leonardo's horse. Akamu, while respecting Leonardo's original vision, also added her unique artistic touch to the project. The end product was not an exact replica of Leonardo's design, but rather a heartfelt homage to his creative genius.

Sadly, Dent passed away in 1994, unable to witness the completion of the project he had so passionately championed. However, his vision didn't die with him. In 1999, the final bronze horse, standing 24 feet tall and weighing 15 tons, was installed in Milan, exactly 500 years after the original clay model was destroyed..

Leonardo's horse at Frederik Meijer Gardens and Sculpture Park in Grand Rapids, Michigan

"The sculpture which I created ... pays homage to the creative genius of Leonardo. It is not intended to be a recreation of his sculpture. However, it has been significantly influenced by certain works of art and writings from that period, and specifically Leonardo's notebooks and accompanying drawings with great emphasis on his involvement with the Sforza monument." ~ Nina Akamu

"Leonardo's Horse" by Nina Akamu in Milan, Italy

Today, Leonardo's Horse stands not only as a tribute to Leonardo da Vinci's genius but also as a testament to the power of perseverance and the timeless beauty of art. It is an enduring reminder that even an unfulfilled dream can inspire future generations to create, innovate, and appreciate the wonder of artistic expression. The story behind Leonardo's horse that never was is a saga of dreams, destruction, discovery, and dedication, proving that sometimes, the journey of creation can be as monumental as the artwork itself.

YASUKE: THE BLACK SAMURAI

In the closing years of the 16th century, Japan, a remarkable figure rose through the ranks of society to become the first black samurai in history. Yasuke, a man of African origin, embarked on an extraordinary journey that saw him forge a lasting place in Japanese lore. His remarkable odyssey, which started in Africa and culminated in Japan, defied racial and societal norms, etching his name on the annals of Japan's feudal past.

From Africa to Japan

Yasuke's fascinating tale unfolded when he was seized from his homeland, believed to be Mozambique, and subsequently enslaved in India. In the book "African Samurai: The True Story of Yasuke, a Legendary Black Warrior in Feudal Japan" co-author Thomas Lockley says Yasuke was probably a free man when he met Alessandro Valignano, a prominent Jesuit missionary who asked Yasuke to accompany him to Japan in 1579 as his bodyguard. In those times missionaries were not allowed to carry weapons and with the turmoil in Japan having a bodyguard in your service was a wise decision. Upon arrival in Kyoto, Yasuke's towering stature and ebony complexion captivated the Japanese, distinguishing him as an enigmatic foreigner.

Captivating Kyoto

When Yasuke arrived in Kyoto, the former capital of Japan, his appearance immediately drew attention. Standing over six feet tall and possessing a strikingly dark complexion, Yasuke captured the curiosity of the public and the ruling elite alike. His unique presence eventually caught the eye of the powerful warlord Oda Nobunaga, who was intrigued by the foreigner's physical prowess and cultural background.

Oda Nobunaga was the preeminent feudal lord and unifying force in Japan at the time, and he quickly forged a strong bond with Yasuke. A story is told that Nobunaga thought Yasuke was covered in black paint and ordered him to be washed, but when his skin remained unchanged, Nobunaga threw a welcome party for the visitor.

Oda Nubunaga (Kanō Sōshū, 1551 - 1601)

Ascension to Samurai

According to historical accounts, Yasuke could speak Japanese and entertained Nobunaga with stories of his homeland and experiences abroad. Impressed by Yasuke's intellect, strength, and loyalty, Nobunaga eventually granted him the prestigious rank of Samurai, making Yasuke the first known black Samurai in Japanese history. This ascension signified Yasuke's trasnformation from an exotic novelty to a revered warrior, a tribute to his exceptional adaptability and the singular rapport he established with the Japanese warlord.

The Samurai Life

As a Samurai, Yasuke's existence was anything but ordinary. He immersed himself in the disciplines of martial arts, equestrianism, and traditional Japanese weaponry, internalizing the revered samurai code of honor; Bushido. As a valued advisor and protector of Nobunaga, Yasuke assumed a pivotal role in Japan's volatile political arena.

He valiantly fought at Nobunaga's side during the Honno-ji Incident of 1582, a crucial confrontation involving the deceit and treachery of Nobunaga's long time ally, Akechi Mitsuhide. As Nobunaga's forces succumbed to the overwhelming forces of Akechi, the lord elected to perform seppuku, a ritualized form of suicide, to evade capture and as a symbolic message of being in control of his own death. The ritual sometimes also involved a kaishakunin or a 'second' who would behead the individual.

It is fabled that after Nobunaga performed seppuku, his deputy decapitated him and Yasuke was given the responsibility of saving Nobunaga's head from enemy capture. If Akechi was to have come into possession of the head it would have given him legitimacy as a ruler. According to Thomas Lockley "Yasuke, therefore, by escaping with the head, could have been seen and has been seen as changing Japanese history."

The Fall and Disappearance

In the wake of Nobunaga's demise, Yasuke's fortunes took a downturn. He allied himself with Oda Nobutada, Nobunaga's son and successor, but was apprehended by Akechi's forces. Yasuke surrendered his sword instead of performing seppuku which in the eyes of Akechi proved that Yasuke was not a true Samuri. Deemed a non-combatant, Yasuke was pardoned from execution and was returned to the Jesuits, subsequently vanishing from historical records.

Enduring Legacy and Lessons

Yasuke's tale offers lessons for us today, embodying the power to overcome racial and cultural challenges to reach remarkable heights. His experiences illustrate how someone can adapt and contribute to a foreign culture while maintaining their distinct identity. Yasuke's journey emphasizes the value of welcoming diversity, as his unique perspective and abilities were essential to his role as a samurai and his service to Nobunaga.

Recently, Yasuke's life has ignited a surge of interest, inspiring books, comics, anime, and an impending live-action Netflix series. This rejuvenated fascination demonstrates the enduring appeal of his story to contemporary audiences and the significance of a narrative that defies traditional norms. Yasuke's saga serves as a powerful testament to the transformative capacity inherent in cross-cultural interactions and the unyielding human potential for valor, commitment, and perseverance.

SECRET APPARTMENT AT THE EIFFEL TOWER

Paris's iconic Eiffel Tower harbors an intriguing secret - a private apartment built solely for the monument's architect Gustave Eiffel to entertain esteemed guests. This exclusive pied-à-terre at the peak of the world's tallest building became the envy of France's elite when revealed. While Eiffel refused to allow anyone to reside there, the apartment's restoration provides a glimpse into his lofty aerie.

Gustave Eiffel's Engineering Marvel

When the Eiffel Tower was erected in 1889 as the entrance arch for the World's Fair, it was the world's tallest manmade structure at 1,063 feet high. Designed by acclaimed engineer Gustave Eiffel, it was initially controversial for it's resemblance to a 'hideous factory chimney,' but later became synonymous with Paris itself.

Eiffel was already renowned for engineering bridges and railway stations when he conceived of the audacious tower proposal. But the Eiffel Tower cemented his legacy as France's "master of metal" and an architect at the forefront of the Industrial Age.

The apartment at the tower's apex reflects Eiffel's scientific mindset. It served as his personal laboratory for conducting experiments, preferable to residing there permanently.

Advertising poster for the 1889 World's Fair in Paris.

Historic photograph of Gustave Eiffel's private
apartment atop the Eiffel Tower

A Coveted Interior High Above Paris

Incorporating an apartment into the design also suggests Eiffel's satisfaction at achieving an unprecedented feat of engineering. At nearly 1,000 feet, his perch far exceeded any luxury residence in Paris.

Unlike the industrial girders and platforms of the public tower, Eiffel's apartment was decorated with wood furnishings, oil paintings, and even a piano. The intimate interior evoked domestic life, hovering in the clouds.

When the apartment's existence became widely known, Paris's elite constantly badgered Eiffel to rent it, even for a single night. But he refused all offers, reserving access only for esteemed guests like Thomas Edison. The apartment's exclusivity and unique vantage fueled public fascination.

Illustration from 1889 of the Eiffel Tower's summit. Originally drawn by M. Rouillard, an engineer that worked with Eiffel on the project.

Speculation on Eiffel's Residence

It's unclear if Eiffel actually resided full-time in the apartment. Some speculate it served more as a comfortable salon for entertainment. The lack of a bedroom seems to confirm the apartment was not meant as a living quarters.

Eiffel reportedly spent a lot of time there conducting meteorological and physics experiments. The apartment's height provided ideal conditions for studies requiring isolation from disruptive vibrations. Eiffel had a laboratory installed nearby to accommodate his research.

For Eiffel, intellectual pursuits in his lofty aerie took priority over lavish living. But hosting luminaries like Edison also fed his ego by showing off the unparalleled views.

Restored Office now Open to Public

These days, visitors can glimpse Eiffel's preserved office near the tower's top, including lifelike wax figures of Eiffel and Edison. While the apartment itself is off limits, the office provides a window into Eiffel's rarified world.

Wax figures of Gustave Eiffel, Thomas Edison and Gustave's daughter, Claire, in the back. They're on public view at Eiffel Tower.

Seeing the furnishings and personal items humanizes the mythic engineer. The apartment's warmth contrasts sharply with the cold industrialism of the surrounding tower. Eiffel's study seems to float in the clouds, suspended between earth and sky.

The apartment captures Eiffel's legacy as both a master builder revering science, and an innovator with flourishes of personality.

Staying in the Eiffel Apartment

While staying in the original apartment is prohibited, occasional contests grant a lucky few the chance to overnight in similar quarters.

In 2016, HomeAway converted an unused top-floor conference room into a temporary vacation apartment. Four winners got to sleep there during the UEFA Euro soccer tournament, enjoying jaw-dropping vistas of Paris.

But no one can replicate Eiffel's experience of residing in the same apartment for decades on end, watching the sunrise from his one-of-a-kind penthouse. The apartment remains unique in the world, befitting the audacious engineer who built the landmark it crowns.

THE LAST WITNESS TO LINCOLN'S ASSASSINATION

On a fateful night in 1865, a young boy of just five years old witnessed one of the most pivotal events in American history – President Abraham Lincoln's assassination. Samuel J. Seymour, who would later recount his experience on the 1956 episode of the TV show "I've Got A Secret," remains the last living witness to this tragic event. Now, over a century later, we delve into Seymour's riveting account and explore the emotions and vivid details of that unforgettable night.

President Lincoln's box at Ford's Theater in Washington, DC 1865

A Young Boy's Fateful Trip

Samuel Seymour's first trip away from home was not one he would ever forget. Accompanied by his father on a business trip to Washington, D.C., the young boy was frightened by the sight of soldiers and guns lining the streets. To help calm his nerves, Seymour's nurse, Sarah Cook, and his godmother, Mrs. Goldsborough, decided to take him to a play at Ford's Theater. Little did they know, this was to be a night that would change the course of history.

The Calm Before the Storm

As the trio settled into their balcony seats across from the presidential box, Seymour's godmother pointed out the colorful flags adorning the box where President Lincoln would be seated. When the tall, whiskered figure of the President finally arrived, he smiled and waved to the audience. This gesture temporarily lifted the somber mood in the theater. As the play, "Our American Cousin," progressed, young Seymour's anxiety gradually eased.

A Child's Perspective: Chaos and Confusion

Confusion and panic swept through the theater, with many audience members unsure of what had transpired. Seymour, too, was bewildered by the turn of events. "I thought there'd been another accident when one man seemed to tumble over the balcony rail and land on the stage," he recalled. Seymour's innocence and compassion shone through as he urged his nurse and godmother to help the man who had fallen. This man was none other than Booth himself, who had injured his leg in the jump.

Illustration of the night of Lincoln's assassination

As pandemonium erupted, cries of "Lincoln's shot! The President's dead!" rang through the air. Mrs. Goldsborough scooped up the young boy and whisked him out of the theater. In his retelling of the event, Seymour revealed that the horror of that night would haunt his dreams for years to come. "That night I was shot 50 times, at least, in my dreams – and I sometimes still relive the horror of Lincoln's assassination, dozing in my rocker as an old codger like me is bound to do," he said.

Seymour's Account

Seymour's account of the assassination, published in the February 7, 1954 issue of The American Weekly, provides a unique and heart-wrenching perspective on the event. There are more detailed recollections of the event from Major Henry Rathbone and others present at Ford's Theater that night. However, Seymour's childlike innocence and naivete offer a touching and humanizing contrast into a tragic moment in American history.

The story of Samuel Seymour resurfaced decades later when he appeared on the CBS TV panel show "I've Got a Secret" on February 9, 1956. Despite suffering a fall prior to the show that left him with a swollen knot above his right eye, Seymour insisted on sharing his story with the nation. Host Garry Moore and the show's producers had urged him to forgo his appearance. However, the resilient witness was determined to recount his experience. Panelists Bill Cullen, Jayne Meadows, and others questioned Seymour. They pieced together his secret connection to the Civil War and the political significance of his story. And in the end, finally, his eyewitness account of Lincoln's assassination.

A Humble Man's Legacy

Seymour's appearance on the show provided a rare opportunity for the American public to hear a firsthand account of Lincoln's assassination from the last living witness. In an era when television was still a relatively new medium, viewers were captivated by the old man's tale.

Samuel J. Seymour

He painted a vivid picture of that fateful night in 1865. As a testament to his humility, Seymour received a can of Prince Albert pipe tobacco from the show's sponsor, R. J. Reynolds Tobacco Company, in lieu of the usual prize of a carton of Winston cigarettes.

Samuel J. Seymour passed away on April 12, 1956, at his daughter's house in Arlington, Virginia. He left behind a legacy of five children, thirteen grandchildren, and 35 great-grandchildren. Today, Seymour rests in Loudoun Park Cemetery in Baltimore, Maryland. His story however, lives on through the accounts he shared in print and on television.

The Power of Storytelling: Transporting Us Back to That Fateful Night

Seymour's poignant and vivid description of Lincoln's assassination stands as a testament to the power of storytelling. It captures the emotion and turmoil of a moment that forever changed the United States. Through his words, we are transported back to that fateful night in Ford's Theater, experiencing the fear, confusion, and heartbreak of a nation in mourning. Moreover, Seymour's account serves as a reminder of the resilience of the human spirit. It also shows the compassion and innocence of a young boy who, despite witnessing a tragedy beyond his comprehension, sought to help a fellow human in need.

Samuel J. Seymour on the popular
T.V. show I've Got a Secret in 1956.

MOST HOSTILE ISLAND IN THE WORLD

Far out in the Indian Ocean lies North Sentinel Island, home to the Sentinelese, one of the most isolated indigenous tribes on Earth. For millennia, the Sentinelese have resisted contact with the outside world, turning away expeditions and sometimes responding violently to protect their way of life. Their steadfast independence has made North Sentinel Island legendary as the most hostile place to outsiders. But the real story behind this remote island reveals a people shaped by isolation, not hostility.

An Island Untouched

North Sentinel Island is located in the Bay of Bengal between India and Myanmar. At only 23 square miles, it is surrounded by coral reefs that act as a natural barrier. The small tropical island lies over 1000 miles from mainland India.

The Sentinelese are believed to have inhabited the island for as long as 60,000 years. Their population likely numbers around 100 individuals divided into bands that stay in different parts of the island. They live in simple thatched huts and survive by fishing, hunting, and gathering wild plants.

Almost nothing is known of the Sentinelese language, beliefs, or customs. They have fiercely prevented any substantial contact by the outside world. Even neighboring indigenous Andaman Islanders have barely interacted with the Sentinelese over centuries. Their complete isolation makes them unique among uncontacted peoples.

Sentinel Island seen from above

Early Encounters: 1880s-1970s

The Sentinelese first became known to the wider world during British colonial rule of India. In 1880, explorer Maurice Vidal Portman led an expedition to North Sentinel Island. When his party approached the island, the Sentinelese hid in the jungle.

After days of searching, Portman's men captured and kidnapped an elderly couple and some children. The older Sentinelese soon died of illness. The outraged British thought it wise to return the orphaned children with gifts. This likely introduced devastating disease and cemented the Sentinelese mistrust of outsiders.

A group of Sentinelese ready to ward off visitors to their island

Over the next century, sporadic attempts were made to contact the reclusive inhabitants. In 1967, a documentary crew was attacked after their grounded vessel drifted onto the reefs surrounding the island. The director took an arrow to his thigh while unloading film equipment.

This did not deter further contact efforts. In 1974, a National Geographic film crew was met with another barrage of arrows. The following year, vessels dropped coconuts as peace offerings, which the Sentinelese buried in the sand.

India's Troubled Contact Program

When India gained independence from Britain in 1947, North Sentinel Island came under Indian control. The government launched an ambitious program to make peaceful contact with the Sentinelese.

From the late 1960s through the 1990s, Indian anthropologist TN Pandit led "gift-dropping" expeditions to the island. Teams would approach North Sentinel in vessels loaded with coconuts, bananas, pigs, dolls, and other goods to demonstrate their friendly intent. But the Sentinelese seldom welcomed these overtures.

During Pandit's 1976 expedition, 35 islanders launched arrows and threw spears at the visiting vessel. Some even squatted in a provocative manner to express their scorn. Pandit's group made brief contact in 1991 when 28 Sentinelese cautiously emerged, but tensions quickly rose again.

Survival International, an indigenous rights organization, protested India's contact efforts as insensitive and reckless. The group argued leaving the Sentinelese alone was the only ethical course. Bowing to criticism, India finally ended the gift drops in the mid-1990s.

The Sentinelese greeting with a bow and arrow

Recent Incidents and an Uncertain Future

In 2006, two Indian fishermen who illegally encroached on the island were killed by the Sentinelese. The men were apparently drunk when their boat drifted onto the reefs during the night. Indian authorities declined to prosecute the tribe, respecting their isolation. Several years later, an American Christian missionary named John Allen Chau met the same fate when he illegally traveled to North Sentinel seeking to convert the tribe. His diary reveals misguided religious zeal, not understanding of Sentinelese customs.

These violent encounters have brought the Sentinelese to global attention. But some anthropologists argue their hostility does not reflect innate aggression - they are defending their home and way of life against invasion.

Nonetheless, modern threats from climate change, disease, and exploitation leave the Sentinelese future uncertain. Their desire to remain isolated poses challenges between cultural preservation and governance. For now, North Sentinel Island remains sealed off to preserve the Sentinelese culture perhaps thousands of years old.

John Allen Chau, the American missionary who snuck onto Sentinel island to proselytize Christianity, but was ultimately killed by the tribe.

Little Known Culture

The extreme isolation of the Sentinelese means the outside world knows next to nothing about their language, beliefs, and customs. From a distance, some basic observations have been made of how the tribe lives:

- Settlements include communal huts and temporary shelters along the coastline. They likely live in small kinship bands.

- Fishing in canoes, gathering wild plants, and hunting are main subsistence activities, using simple tools and weapons like bows and arrows.

- They craft shallow outrigger canoes for fishing in the coastal waters and gathering seafood like clams.

- Coconut palms and other tropical foliage provide building materials for rudimentary thatched dwellings.

- They appear healthy, active, and thriving in their traditional hunter-gatherer lifestyle.

But beyond these rudimentary details gleaned from afar, the Sentinelese culture remains a mystery cloaked by the island's isolation. Their language and rituals are unknown, lost to the world outside their remote shoreline home.

Protecting The Sentinelese Isolation

The Indian government currently enforces strict protections and exclusions zones around North Sentinel Island to preserve the Sentinelese way of life. The laws aim to deter intruders and prevent exploitation.

Legislation prohibits going within 5 nautical miles of the island, photographing the tribe, or attempting to make contact. The Andaman and Nicobar Protection of Aboriginal Tribes Regulation of 1956, amended periodically, provides the main legal framework protecting indigenous islanders like the Sentinelese.

However, some argue the isolation policies still don't give the Sentinelese true self-determination or ability to engage the outside world on their terms. Survival International contends the Sentinelese should be granted rights to their surrounding seas and coasts to control their own destiny.

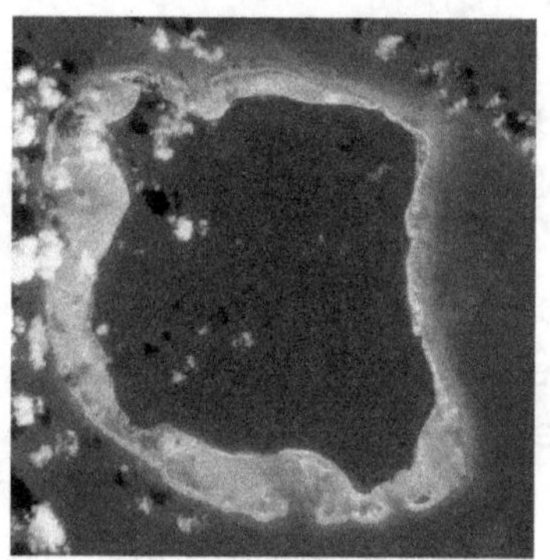

Sentinel Island surrounded by coral reefs as a natural barrier. A three mile long border

But with deep mistrust of outsiders and no resistance to modern diseases, contact comes with real risks. The Sentinelese must navigate preserving their culture amidst changing times under policies made for them, but not by them. Their future, like their island, remains isolated.

JAPANESE REALITY SHOW THAT WENT TOO FAR

Japan has a long fascination with eccentric game shows and reality TV concepts that often perplex Western audiences. But in the late 1990s, one show took this spectacle to alarming new heights, highlighting serious ethical risks of exploitation in entertainment.

The program "Susunu! Denpa Shonen" subjected participants to extreme isolation and deprivation all while filming their suffering as comedy fodder for millions of viewers.

The story of contestant Nasubi and his traumatic experience on the show reveals the darker side of reality television and the line between humor and inhumanity.

Outrageous Japanese Reality TV

Japanese game shows have mystified outsiders for decades with wacky premises like having people identify chocolate candies while blindfolded or get hit in the crotch when messing up tongue twisters. Shows like "Endurance" combined bizarre challenges like chugging hot sauce then immediately sniffing spicy mustard.

But some concepts went beyond just silly and verge into the realm of torture. "Troop of 100" had 100 people spontaneously chase an unsuspecting person on the street, leaving them rattled. "How to Escape a Fart" involved contestants spreading dyed gas around a room.

While these may have been ratings hits, a controversial new show emerged in 1998 that took things even further. "Susunu! Denpa Shonen" subjected participants to demeaning, dangerous, and psychologically damaging situations all in the name of spectacle.

The Premis of "Susunu! Denpa Shonen"

Every season of "Susunu! Denpa Shonen" had a different survival-style concept aimed at attracting viewers through shocking hardships. Contestants had to hitchhike across Africa or escape a deserted island with no supplies.

But one segment in particular drew the most attention - "Sweepstakes Life" featuring aspiring comedian Nasubi. The premise? Place Nasubi alone in an apartment with nothing but magazines. He had to survive only on prizes won by entering magazine sweepstakes until he reached $10,000 in winnings.

Tomoaki Hamatsu - Japanese comedian

Producers stripped Nasubi naked and left him no clothes, food, or any outside contact. His real name was Tomoaki Hamatsu, but he was dubbed "Nasubi" as his genitals were covered by an animated eggplant for viewers, due to his nudity. This is also the origin of why the 'eggplant' emoji is now associated with the phallus.

For nearly a year, while supposedly entering over 1,400 sweepstakes a week, Nasubi starved in isolation as the camera filmed constantly. He believed he was self-recording footage that might air later. But in reality, his daily life was being broadcast nationally with mocking sound effects added.

At-Home Humiliation

As Nasubi slowly won meager prizes like dog food or rice to survive, the show depicted his progress - and emotional breakdowns - as comedy entertainment. He was denied any clothes besides lingerie, leaving him naked the entire time. Loneliness and starvation took an obvious toll as his speech slowed and he talked to inanimate objects.

Millions tuned in to watch the public exploitation and humiliation of Nasubi. In a country one-third the size, it broke ratings records at 17 million regular viewers.

But as a foreign audience, most felt not amusement but moral revulsion. What could possibly be funny about human suffering manufactured for spectacle? Yet Japan was enthralled.

Tomoaki Hamatsu AKA Nasubi talking to a stuffed animal, in a sparse room without clothes, surrounded by magazines. He spent over 15 months in isolation like this.

After 335 days surviving on his winnings, Nasubi finally reached the monetary goal. But producers cruelly moved him to an identical apartment in Korea, telling him to win enough to return home. Already traumatized, Nasubi suffered further before earning another ticket back.

When he arrived in Japan, Nasubi was again placed in a duplicate apartment and told to undress. Suddenly the walls collapsed - revealing a studio audience surrounding him. After 15 months isolated, this public spectacle pushed Nasubi to the brink. He was completely baffled as hosts explained millions had watched his degradation as entertainment for over a year.

Lasting Damage

Unsurprisingly, Nasubi exited the show scarred. He struggled holding conversations for months after being deprived of human contact. For a year, wearing clothes made him sweaty and uncomfortable. The hopeful comedian had become an unwilling reality star, left to handle the fame he never desired.

Nasubi in the visual novel adventure game "428 Shibuya Scramble"

Yet when the show's producer was confronted years later about Nasubi's obvious trauma, he expressed no regret. He even disturbingly claimed it was "thrilling" to witness the "miracle" of human struggle recorded on film. Clearly no concern existed for contestants' well-being.

But Nasubi has worked hard not to let those scars define him. In 2016, he climbed Mount Everest after several failed attempts, crediting the mental fortitude built through his harsh ordeal. And he continues performing comedy and acting today. Still, the show clearly extracted a heavy price.

The Appeal and Ethics of Reality TV Suffering

Nasubi's experience poses uncomfortable questions about the line between entertainment and exploitation. Why do brutal reality shows attract such devotion? What drives the appeal of spectacles showcasing human pain?

Observers highlight voyeurism and the schadenfreude of enjoying others' adversity. Watching people debased for amusement triggers our cruelest impulses. And Nasubi's innocence in displaying unfiltered emotion - without realizing he was mocked by millions - made the show irresistible.

But as reality contests become more extreme, ethical concerns grow. Even shows like Survivor and Fear Factor profit off degradation. And subjects can suffer inhuman treatment yet have no power against the enterprise built around their suffering.

Many defend this as merely "fake" staging. But trauma still inflicts real damage, physically and mentally, regardless of context contrived for cameras. And fans are complicit in incentivizing intensifying brutality. Nasubi's story illustrates the tipping point past which human dignity becomes expendable for ratings, putting superficial fun ahead of empathy.

Reality television will likely continue mining prurient impulses. But understanding what participants undergo for our idle entertainment is vital. Perhaps Nasubi's unthinkable isolation and abuse can teach that no fleeting diversion justifies the long-term costs of manufactured human distress. The spectacle may entertain, but we must reconcile its inhumanity.

WAR WIDOW WHO DIED 155 YEARS AFTER WAR

When Helen Viola Jackson passed away in December 2020 at age 101, it marked the end of an era. She was the last known surviving widow of a Civil War veteran, dying over 155 years after the war concluded.

Her quiet marriage to 93-year-old James Bolin in 1936 connected her to one of America's bloodiest conflicts even into the modern day. Helen's incredible life story illustrates the surprising legacies that can persist through time.

A Teenage Bride

Helen was born in 1919 and raised on a small farm in Missouri along with 9 siblings. She first met her future husband, James Bolin, at church in the early 1930s. Bolin was a Civil War veteran in his 90s who had served as a private in the Union Army.

Helen Viola Jackson in 1955

After her father volunteered Helen, then 17, to assist the widower Bolin with household chores, the elder man soon proposed. As Helen later recalled, Bolin offered a pragmatic reason, saying: "He said that he would leave me his Union pension. It was during the depression and times were hard. He said that it might be my only way of leaving the farm."

On September 4, 1936, Helen and James married in an intimate ceremony at his home. Despite the 76-year age gap, Helen held her husband in high regard: "Mr. Bolin really cared for me. He wanted me to have a future and he was so kind." Though technically wed, Helen continued using her maiden name and residing with her parents - an unconventional union even then.

Secret Marriage Lasts 3 Years

Keenly aware of wagging tongues, Helen guarded her marriage's privacy for decades. As she stated in one interview: "I had great respect for Mr. Bolin, and I did not want him to be hurt by the scorn of wagging tongues." Helen also feared damage to her own reputation as a young woman apparently marrying solely for financial reasons.

So she hid the marriage nearly all her life, telling only a few witnesses who attended the wedding. James Bolin passed away in 1939 after 3 years of technically being Helen's husband. Even into old age, she never claimed his promised pension, denying rumors she exploited an elderly man. For over 75 years, Helen's brief marriage remained a closely held secret only revealed privately near her death.

James Bolin was in the cavalry in the Civil War
and married Jackson from 1936 until his death in 1939

Helen's union, though unique, was not the only marriage between a young woman and aged veteran in the early 20th century. Economic instability often motivated teen brides and aging grooms to wed. Three other teen brides also became Civil War widows by marrying octogenarians:

- Maudie Hopkins, 19, married 86-year-old Confederate veteran William Cantrell in 1934

- Alberta Martin, 21, married 81-year-old Confederate soldier William Jasper Martin in 1927

- Gertrude Janeway, 17, married 81-year-old Union veteran John Janeway in 1934

Like Helen, these women tied their lives to aging Civil War veterans in the 1930s. Passage of time ultimately connected them all to the 19th century conflict through their husbands. These May-December marriages became a path to financial security in trying times.

William Cantrell and his wife Maudie (later Hopkins in 1936. Their ages, about 88 and 21.

No Pension Despite Widow Status

Though Helen was legally Bolin's widow, she never capitalized on the promised military pension after his passing. One of Bolin's daughters threatened to tarnish Helen's reputation if she pursued the pension. In Helen's own words: "All a woman had in 1939 was her reputation. I didn't want them all to think that I was a young woman who had married an old man to take advantage of him."

So despite being low on money, Helen refrained from applying as a matter of principle. For decades, she even hid the marriage itself to avoid gossip. Only in her late 90s did Helen privately confirm her role as James Bolin's widow, showing both the stigma she felt and personal nature of her story.

Embracing Her Place in History

In the final years of her life, Helen increasingly embraced her unique position in history. While she still valued privacy, Helen allowed her marriage to James Bolin to be verified by Civil War heritage associations. She gifted Bolin's engraved Bible, which recorded their union, to a museum exhibit.

Helen also welcomed letters and cards from well-wishers, a contrast to her prior discreet nature. She enjoyed recognition from local Missouri organizations highlighting her special status as the last person still directly connected to the Civil War. For Helen, separating fact from fiction regarding her marriage became important only late in life.

Jackson was an honored guest at the Memorial Day celebration at the National Cemetery in Springfield, MO, in November 2018

Passing of a Private Figure

The rediscovery of Helen's role as the final Civil War widow sheds light on a woman who purposely avoided the limelight most of her life. Helen preferred keeping her notable marriage closely guarded rather than risk gossip. That someone with such a singular place in history valued privacy first speaks volumes about her character.

In her final years, Helen allowed her story to be shared on her own terms. She demonstrated that even an event as profound as the Civil War could still touch the lives of individuals over a century later. Though Helen has passed, her principles and resilience will remain inspiring.

Remembering the Civil War's Human Impact

The American Civil War ended over 155 years ago, yet Helen's life demonstrated how wars continue impacting people long after the final battles conclude. The war's legacy rippled into the 20th century through Helen's marriage to James Bolin, reminding us of the Civil War's immense human toll.

Other individuals further exemplify the war's lasting effects. Irene Triplett, who died in 2020, was the final person still receiving a Civil War pension as the child of a veteran. And in 1959, the last verified widower of a Revolutionary War bride passed away, underscoring how wars reverberate through generations.

Helen's passing severs one of our last living links to the Civil War. It represents a symbolic turning point as the world moves further away from a defining 19th century conflict. Helen's choice to finally share her remarkable story provides insight into a war that still touches America today.

Painting: The Girl I Left Behind by Eastman
Johnson, 1872, Smithsonian American Art Museum
This famous Civil War painting by Johnson
features a young, beautiful girl left waiting for her
husband to return as she looks down from atop a
high hilltop.

The Ripple Effects of War

Wars reshape societies and change individual lives irrevocably. The Civil War brought immense loss and upheaval, emancipating enslaved people but also leaving over 600,000 dead. Widows like Helen dealt with the war's consequences rippling into peacetime.

Figures like the last soldier, widow or child allow us to measure wars' longevity. Today, the final World War I veterans have passed. But other survivors maintain connections, reminding us of how political events transform human stories. Helen's marriage to James connected her to seismic 19th century events late into the modern era.

By binding her life to Civil War history, Helen provided a tangible link between the past and present. Her passing represents both the war's fading from living memory and how its legacies still reach into the nation's future. Remembering figures like Helen helps humanity reflect on the true costs of war.

The Search for Financial Security

What motivated Helen's unusual marriage to the nonagenarian Bolin? Though barely more than a child herself, the Great Depression left Helen struggling to support her future. Marrying the older widower offered potential escape through a military pension if Helen cared for him until his death.

Other teen brides like Helen faced similar hardships and saw marriage to elderly veterans as a path to financial security. Though not based on romance, these unions allowed women to survive challenging circumstances while providing comfort to aging vets.

Helen maintained affection and respect for her husband despite their age gap. Her pragmatic decision provided a lifeline in desperate times, even if unconventional. The marriage attests to the extreme actions that widespread hardship forced upon youth like Helen.

Lasting Legacies of Teen Brides By marrying aged veterans, Helen and her counterparts gained means for survival. They also became the last living bridges between the 19th and 21st centuries. Though most endured gossip rather than fame, these women passed quietly into history after World War II.

Helen's secret marriage left her identity as the final Civil War widow hidden until her dying days. But other teenage brides from the era likewise connected our modern times to the 1800s by the barest threads. Their incredible longevity serves as a reminder of war's lingering trauma.

Through her marriage to a nonagenarian Civil War veteran, Helen inextricably tied her life to one of America's bloodiest conflicts. By revealing her remarkable story, she demonstrated war's ability to transcend lifetimes and touch even future generations. Though Helen has passed, her legacy persists as a symbol of war's human impacts over time.

Helen Jackson sits with portrait o her husband, a Civil War Veteran.

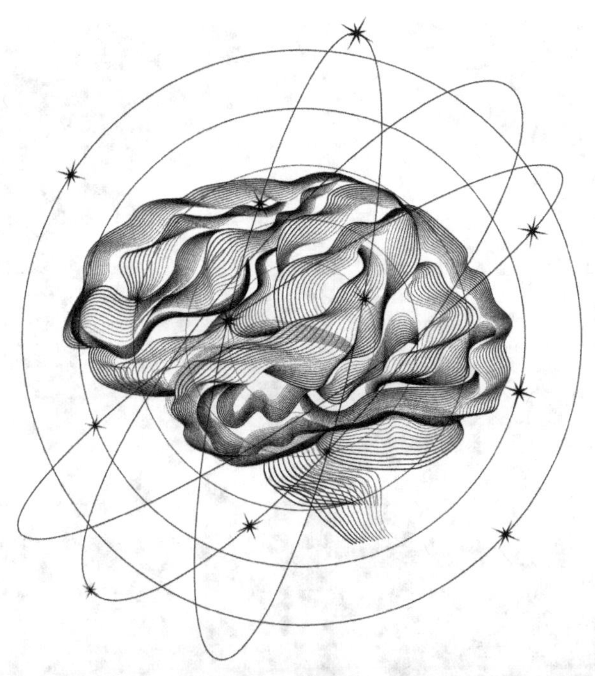

THE MAN WHO STOLE EINSTEIN'S BRAIN

Albert Einstein is undoubtedly one of the greatest scientific minds in history. The German-born physicist developed the theory of relativity, which revolutionized our understanding of time, space, gravity, and the universe. His famous equation $E=mc2$ demonstrated the equivalence of mass and energy and laid the foundation for nuclear power. Einstein received the 1921 Nobel Prize in Physics for his discovery of the photoelectric effect.

Beyond his scientific brilliance, Einstein was known for his pacifism, liberal politics, and advocacy for a Jewish homeland. His daring escape from Nazi Germany to the United States made him an international celebrity. Einstein was regularly consulted on ethical and political issues and rubbed shoulders with the likes of Charlie Chaplin. His tousled appearance and charming personality added to his icon status. There's no doubt Einstein's intellectual gifts made him a genius of the 20th century.

The Death of a Legend

On April 18, 1955, Einstein experienced severe pain from a ruptured abdominal aortic aneurysm. At the Princeton Hospital, the 76-year-old refused invasive surgery, saying "It is tasteless to prolong life artificially. I have done my share, it is time to go." Later that day, the world-renowned scientist passed away peacefully in the hospital with his colleagues by his side.

Einstein did not want a funeral or for his body to be worshipped. He left instructions to be cremated and have his ashes scattered secretly. But Dr. Thomas Harvey, the pathologist who performed the autopsy, had other plans.

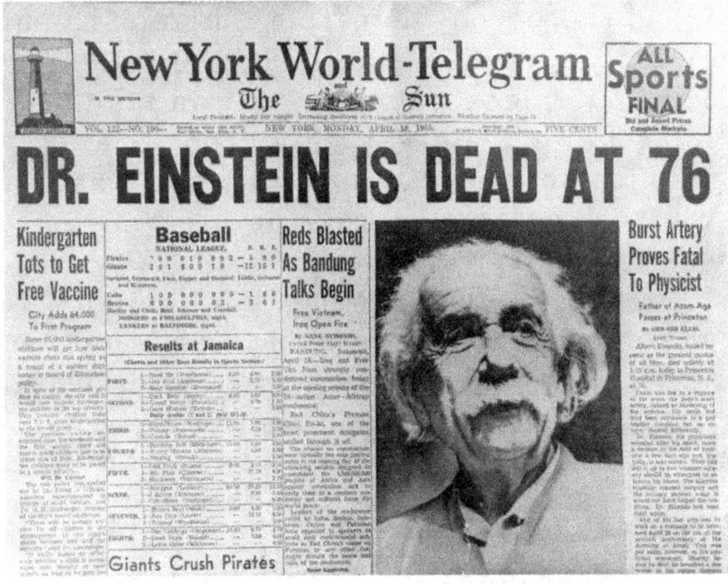

Dr. Thomas Hardy

The Theft of a Celebrated Mind

Against Einstein's wishes, Dr. Harvey decided to preserve the physicist's brain for scientific study. He removed the organ and kept it without initial permission from Einstein's family. Harvey photographed and dissected the brain into over 200 pieces, hoping to gain insight into Einstein's genius. Harvey reflected, "I knew we had permission to do an autopsy, and I assumed that we were going to study the brain."

Unfortunately, this assumption would cost Harvey his job. The removal was front page news the next day, generating headlines like "Doctor Takes Einstein's Brain." As neither Einstein nor his family had consented to the unusual act, Harvey faced serious repercussions. He was dismissed from Princeton Hospital on grounds that he had violated the autopsy protocol.

Harvey was determined to continue studying the brain, believing the anatomy held the key to Einstein's intellect. So he kept the dissected remains, which he had preserved in celloidin, a rubbery type of cellulose. Harvey placed the pieces of Einstein's brain into two glass jars and relocated to Philadelphia. This time, he had permission from Einstein's son Hans Albert, provided that any investigation was only conducted for scientific purposes. But Harvey would soon find studying the historic brain in his basement was easier said than done.

The Hidden Brain

Over the next four decades, Thomas Harvey struggled to find researchers interested in examining Einstein's brain. As he lacked expertise in neuroscience himself, Harvey needed to partner with the right scientists to gain insight from the organ. But the pathologist found it difficult to convince specialists of the value in analyzing a single brain without comparisons.

There were also few legal options at the time for obtaining control brains for comparison. Additionally, Harvey's conduct had been publicly scrutinized, making many in the research community wary. As interest and funding failed to materialize, Harvey's treasured specimen remained mostly confined to storage.

Dr. Harvey with Einstein's Brain

Between New Jersey, Missouri, Kansas, and back again, Harvey transported Einstein's brain bits in nondescript containers, tucked away from the public eye. At one point, his wife threatened to dispose of the bothersome brain pieces. For decades, the historic organ stayed stowed away in basements, hidden in beer coolers and cider boxes, as Harvey struggled to unlock its secrets.

Questionable Science

Finally, in the 1980s, over 30 years after Einstein's death, Thomas Harvey partnered with scientists willing to study the preserved cerebral matter. His first collaborators were researchers at the University of California, Berkeley. In 1985, the team published the first examination of Einstein's brain in the journal Experimental Neurology.

Using celloidin-embedded slide samples Harvey provided, the authors claimed Einstein's brain had an abnormally low neuron-to-glia ratio in the region known as Brodmann area 39. Glia are cells that support and protect neurons. The researchers speculated this distinctive cellular makeup might explain Einstein's mathematical and spatial skills. However, the small control sample of 11 brains and lack of blinded cell counting raised considerable criticism.

More questionable studies soon followed. Harvey joined with Alabama scientists to count neurons in Einstein's frontal cortex from digitized photos, declaring the region was thinner than average. Canadian researchers also obtained photos of Einstein's brain that Harvey had collected prior to dissection. Comparing surface features, that team conjectured Einstein's unusual parietal lobe anatomy could underlie his mathematical talents.

But all these studies were fundamentally flawed. They relied on tiny samples of the brain, inappropriate control groups, and measurements that were not blinded. The researchers frequently lacked expertise in pathology and made unsupported leaps between anatomy and intelligence. Overall, the science behind Einstein's stolen brain failed to deliver conclusive insights.

Controversial Samples

Seeking to further investigate Einstein's neurobiology, Harvey divided up portions of the brain to mail off to researchers across the globe. He hoped disseminating samples would help achieve his dream of learning what made Einstein tick. In addition to sending slices to Berkeley, Harvey parceled out bits of cerebrum to specialists in Toronto, New York, and even Japan.

However, not all recipients handled the samples ethically. One of the Japanese researchers kept the rare chunk of Einstein's brain he was loaned rather than returning it. The brain portions mailed overseas became subject to legal disputes over rightful ownership. Harvey himself even came under investigation for transporting the specimens outside the U.S. without proper documents.

Sharing samples internationally enabled more scientists to probe the mysteries of Einstein's mind.

But it came at an ethical cost and yielded controversial results. Studies on the brain chunks showed a range of alleged anomalies - more compact neurons, thicker cortex, expanded glial cells. Yet issues with tiny samples and lack of blinded controls persisted. The investigations sparked debates about interpreting brain anatomy without an owner's permission. In the end, the fantastical research failed to definitively reveal correlates of Einstein's aptitude.

Einstein's Brain in a Jar

The Failures of Phrenology

Why did decades of microscopic analyses on Albert Einstein's stolen brain fail to illuminate the source of his imaginative genius? As it turns out, reducing the seat of a man's intellect to bits of flesh in jars is an endeavor doomed to futility. Einstein himself warned: "not everything that counts can be counted."

The pseudo-scientific studies on Einstein's brain hark back to the days of phrenology. This antiquated theory claimed that localized brain regions controlled specific talents like language, logic, or music. Phrenologists read head bumps to decipher mental strengths. But modern neuroscience reveals that human cognition arises from distributed neural networks, not particular areas.

Of course, there are singularities to Einstein's life experience that shaped his breakthroughs. His personality, upbringing, encounters with nature, and education formed meaningful patterns within his brain. But these connections can't be gleaned from slivers of dead cells. In the end, the crude grave robbery and dissection of Einstein's brain failed to capture the ineffable spark of genius it once cradled. The ill-begotten samples served only as a potent reminder that our minds transcend mere matter.

The Afterlife of a Brilliant Organ

What became of Einstein's brain after this frenzied period of misguided research? In the 1990s, Thomas Harvey returned the remainder of the brain to Princeton Hospital. A pathologist named Elliott Krauss took over stewardship, promising to protect the organ's dignity. Most of the brain pieces were preserved in formaldehyde, while Einstein's eyes stayed in a safe deposit box.

When Krauss died in 2007, he passed the baton to another pathologist, Michael Paterniti. Einstein's brain pieces were relocated to Paterniti's lab in New Jersey. Photos leaked in 2010, showing crinkled grey matter in old glass jars. Scientifically useless but historically precious, the specimens remain sequestered from public view.

The saga of Einstein's purloined brain underscores how even men of conscience can rationalize questionable acts in hopes of advancing knowledge. Yet the folly of Harvey's endeavor proves the limitations of reducing genius to biology.

Movie released in 2023 about Einstein's brain

Einstein's true legacy lives on not through remnants of his anatomy, but through the boundless creativity he unleashed in life. As Einstein mused, "The most beautiful thing we can experience is the mysterious." His greatest ideas echo through spacetime not because of brain matter, but the metaphysical matter of his mind.

THE HORSE DUNG DILEMMA OF 1894

In the late 1800s, cities faced a smelly crisis that seemed unsolvable. Streets were choking on the massive quantities of manure left behind by the thousands of horses essential for transport and shipping. With no solution in sight, some declared that urban civilization was doomed to be smothered in horse waste. Yet the great manure calamity never came to pass, offering a cautionary tale about crying doom too readily.

A City Drowning in Dung

In 1894, life in thriving metropolises like London and New York City centered around horses. Long before cars, people relied on hansom cabs and omnibuses pulled by teams of horses to get around. Freight wagons and drays drawn by the animals transported produce, parcels, and goods across muddy streets.

London's 11,000 cabs and several thousand buses each needed fresh horses working in shifts to operate. This added up to over 50,000 horses transporting Londoners daily. Meanwhile, New York's 100,000+ horses produced nearly 2.5 million pounds of manure and 10 million gallons of urine per day.

As cities expanded, ever more horses were pressed into service, which created a messy crisis. Horse manure and carcasses accumulated on streets, along with thriving flies that spread disease. The noxious issue grew into a public health nightmare.

Doomsday Predictions

In 1894, the Times of London gloomily predicted that within 50 years every street would be buried under 9 feet of manure. The situation seemed dire, especially when the first urban planning conference held in 1898 ended abruptly after failing to generate solutions.

With horse numbers increasing and land for disposal shrinking, bacteria-laden manure was creating intolerable urban environments. The crisis laid bare the limits of planning in rapidly growing cities. There seemed no way for public health, transit, and sanitation to keep pace with booming populations and inadequate infrastructure.

Humorists joked that cities would need to construct second or third stories for their sidewalks. With no relief in sight, many saw the writing on the wall - urban civilization faced an existential threat from horse waste accumulating unchecked.

Easter morning 1900: 5th Ave, New York City. Spot the automobile.

Easter morning 1913: 5th Ave, New York City. Spot the horse.

Source: George Grantham Bain Collection.

Crisis Spurs Innovation

Necessity is the mother of invention, and the manure predicament sparked new thinking. Rising costs of feeding, housing, and disposing of waste forced innovation in street transit. Electric trams and motorized buses gradually replaced horse-drawn transport.

But the real solution galloped in as Henry Ford's automobile assembly line debuted the Model T - the first affordable car for many families. As cars became accessible to the middle class, public interest shifted from public to private transport. Cities eagerly paved over cobblestone streets to accommodate automobiles.

Within decades, cars outnumbered horses even in congested Manhattan. The last horse-pulled streetcar was retired in 1917. Practically overnight, the manure problem vanished as horses were replaced. Long-predicted urban collapse was avoided through technology and changing habits.

Panic Peddling?

In hindsight, manure panic seems short-sighted. But grave concerns were valid, given knowledge and tools available in the late 1800s. With cities rapidly expanding and infrastructure agging, public health risks were real.

However, critics note that declared inevitable disasters often fail to account for society's ability to adapt. Human ingenuity will usually create solutions if given the right incentives and freedom to respond. Innovation and changing attitudes, not centralized planning, alleviated the waste crisis.

Of course, cars brought their own headaches in pollution, traffic, and suburban sprawl. But they stimulated American industry and offered personal freedoms. trade-offs still debated today.

Risk of Complacency

Does the manure miscalculation hold lessons today? Alarmist language pervades issues like climate change, warning of civilizational collapse if trends continue unchecked.

Perhaps crises seem more insoluble in modern society. But declaring defeat through projections invite self-fulfilling prophecies. People may abandon hope and feel helpless in the face of supposed inevitabilities.

The Model T, sold by the Ford Motor Company from 1908 to 1927
Between 1913 and 1927, Ford factories produced
more than 15 million Model Ts.

This mindset can become justification for restrictive policies that curb freedoms and imperil open inquiry. Yet breakthroughs often emerge from unplanned corners. Brilliant solutions start with believing they exist.

The manure panic shows even trends that appear inexorably disastrous can reverse through human ingenuity. But this relies on preserving conditions where inspiration can flourish, not smothering society in defeatism.

Future shocks will emerge. But civilization has overcome seemingly existential threats before, like mountains of manure filling London's streets. Rather than Fearmongering figuratively and literally, faith in creative spirit may drive solutions.

The Next Crisis Catalyst?

What modern "manure crisis" is awaiting an unforeseen breakthrough? Climate change, environmental pollution, sustainable energy sources, and emerging technologies like AI all pose complex challenges, but frameable as existential threats.

Perhaps hydrogen provides a cleaner fuel alternative. Or lab-grown meat eliminates factory farming. Or carbon capture progresses beyond infancy. An obscure patent application today may contain the seed of resolution, like Carl Benz's 1886 "vehicle powered by a gas engine" that ushered in motoring.

But the seeds of great inventions only flourish in fertile ground. Problem-solvers require economic and intellectual freedom to experiment and spread concepts. Even ideas that seem eccentric or unrealistic merit exploring without stigma.

The lessons of the manure panic are that challenges viewed as insurmountable can disappear nearly overnight, and stagnation arises only when imagining better futures ceases. With openness and courage, society can clear paths through the thorniest modern problems as innovators once cleanly swept horse droppings into history's dustbin.

THE MANEATER OF CHAMPAWAT

In the Himalayan foothills at the turn of the 20th century, an unsettling quiet fell upon a string of villages dotting the forested landscape. An ominous chill took hold as locals ceased venturing beyond their doors. Those who dared set foot outside risked a gruesome demise with little warning. For a ruthless serial killer lurked in the shadows - not a deranged human, but a wounded tigress with a taste for human flesh.

What drove the "Tiger Queen's" bloody 7-year rampage across northern India? How could one elusive beast evade capture and spread such horror? And who finally ended her reign of terror that claimed over 400 lives? Hers is a harrowing tale of the complex relationship between man and nature's apex predators. One that still haunts the region over a century later.

Nepal's Phantom Killer

Our grim story begins in the western hills of Nepal circa 1898. In the quiet district of Rupal, the first faint stirrings of unease took hold as villagers started disappearing into the forest. The occasional mauling was known to happen in these parts. But soon the attacks accelerated at an alarming pace. Twenty here. Fifty there. Bodies turned up mauled and half-eaten. It became apparent that no one who ventured near the treeline was safe.

Hunting parties were dispatched to track down the killer lurking in the shadows. But the cunning beast outwitted them at every turn, evading traps and gunfire. Her phantom-like presence continued to haunt the periphery of remote villages lining the hillsides. Speculation brewed that multiple maneater tigers were to blame for the attacks spread over such a vast territory.

In reality, the killer was frighteningly real and

The Mighty Bengal Tiger

shockingly just a single female Bengal tiger. Even with hundreds perishing, she remained maddeningly invisible. But simply by listening for the spine-chilling roar echoing from the forests, the villagers knew...the maneater was still out there. And she was famished.

Driven by Hunger

By 1905, the elusive tigress had claimed over 200 lives in western Nepal. Finally, the Nepalese army joined the hunt in full force. Soldiers scoured the forests as the kill count rose. After months of relentlessly tracking their forests, the army patrols tightened the noose, denying the tiger access to prey. Starving her out at last, they pressed the tigress downhill toward the Sarda River and the Indian border.

And so began the most notorious killing spree

in history. Crossing into India's Kumaon district, the crippled Bengal tiger found a new hunting ground teeming with vulnerable prey. She adapted quickly, traveling 20 miles between kills, cleverly avoiding the villages roused by her latest victim. Reports trickled in as the tigress claimed three...five...eight lives a day. Mostly women and children foraging the forests fell prey.

Jim Corbett

In this way, the elusive serial killer evaded the bounty hunters dispatched to claim the 1,000 rupee reward on her head. The villages under attack, their livelihoods paralyzed by fear, grew desperate for a savior. Little did the settlers know, the key to their salvation lay in a chance encounter some years prior.

Jim Corbett VS The Tiger Queen

As the most prolific hunter in the region, Jim Corbett was no stranger to tracking man-eating big cats. Years earlier, he had actually crossed paths with the Champawat tiger before her taste for human flesh fully developed. While walking through the forest, Corbett startled the tigress feeding on a buffalo calf. Avoiding his rifle fire, the tiger fled and vanished, leaving a lasting impression on Corbett.

Now the settlers' cries for help echoed as a grim calling, and Corbett felt compelled to respond. Upon arriving in Champawat district in 1907, he recognized the tiger's trademark killing style from the casualties still mounting. Though Corbett preferred to hunt alone, even he knew the clever Champawat maneater demanded special tactics.

For the first time, Corbett organized a beat of over 300 villagers to help corner his crafty adversary. Driven from her lair toward the waiting guns, the trail of blood left by her latest kill allowed the team to anticipate her movements. After declaring he would "either shoot the tigress or the tigress would shoot me," Jim Corbett readied for the confrontation of a lifetime.

Jim Corbett building a machan hayrick during
an earlier hunt for the leopard of Rudraprayag.

The Hunt Climaxes at Dusk

On a fateful spring evening in 1907, the manhunt reached its dramatic climax. Lured by gunshots and cries echoing through the forest, the maneater emerged from the brush at dusk. But rather than fleeing the commotion, she fearlessly charged head-on toward Jim Corbett and the local tahsildar.

Corbett's first shots struck the frenzied tigress in the chest and shoulder. But still she thundered closer, hellbent on taking Corbett with her. With his final bullet, Corbett caught her limping charge in the foot just 20 feet away. The tigress crashed to the forest floor, her long reign of terror definitively over.

In a cruel twist of irony, examination of the slain tiger revealed that the upper and lower canine teeth on her right had been shattered long ago by a careless poacher's bullet. No longer able to catch natural prey, she was left weakened and starving until discovering an easier meal - humans. Forced into desperation by her injury, over seven years she had killed and eaten over 400 men, women and children.

At long last, Jim Corbett had freed the terrified villages of northern India from the bloody clutches of the "Tiger Queen." But for Corbett, still holding the spent rifle that felled the maneater, the socioeconomic plot lines tying hunters, habitat loss and starving predators began coming into sharp focus.

Picture of Champawat Maneater's Head in a newspaper clipping

A New Mission Takes Shape

In the years following his successful hunt, Jim Corbett transitioned from celebrated hunter into a devoted conservationist. Haunted by the fate of the crippled tigress that claimed so many lives, Corbett grew wary of unchecked trophy hunting devastating India's Bengal tiger population.

He pivoted from stalking wildlife through gun sights to capturing tigers' glory through his camera lens instead. The renderings would illustrate Corbett's new mission - raising awareness about India's vanishing habitats and the protection of endangered species, especially its national icon - Panthera tigris tigris.

Jim Corbett's photo album

Corbett played an instrumental role in establishing India's first national park, Hailey National Park, in 1936. Today known as Corbett Tiger Reserve, the preserve promotes conservation of the Bengal tiger and countless other species.

In this way, the trauma left by the Champawat maneating tiger catalyzed Corbett's calling to defend India's great cats rather than hunt them. And Corbett Tiger Reserve remains a living legacy to that transformation today.

Books authored by Jim Corbett on his adventures in the jungle

Enduring Legacy of the Champawat Maneater

The remarkable 12-year saga of the Champawat maneater tiger came to a decisive end that evening in 1907 beneath Jim Corbett's smoking rifle. But the incredible events spawned a legend that still echoes through the region over a century later.

The sheer audacity displayed by the wounded tigress inspires both shock and grudging awe. That even a handicapped apex predator could so easily unleash havoc highlights the delicate balance between man and beast. And Corbett's own reckoning shows how profoundly confronting such forces can reshape one's purpose entirely.

So the tragic events that unfolded in the shadows of the Himalayan foothills still provide relevant lessons today. From the fruits borne of Corbett's tireless activism to the humbling might displayed by nature's perfect hunters when backed into a corner, the echoes still resonate. And the name Champawat is sure to endure for centuries more as a cautionary tribute to the most prolific maneater ever known.

TREADMILL TORTURE

Glancing at the treadmills lined up in your gym, you'd never guess the sinister backstory behind this popular workout machine. Before treadmills built athletes, they brutally punished prisoners. Those first "treadwheels" crippled inmates for months through endless monotonous climbing. So how exactly did appliances designed to shatter convicts become today's go-to fitness equipment? The surprising journey reveals dark origins we forget each time we "dreadmill" in the gym.

A Tool for Torture

Our story opens in 19th century Britain. Rising crime plagued cities and idleness corrupted prisons. Seeking solutions in 1818, Sir William Cubitt devised an imposing wooden wheel covered in isolated compartments for inmates. Up to 40 prisoners at once stepped upwards in place for hours powering its rotation. This endless "everlasting staircase" aimed crushing inmates' will through toilsome labor.

Dubbed the "treadwheel," Cubitt's torture device became widely deployed for reforming criminals. Oscar Wilde penned an agonized poem after two years treading a wheel shredded his health. But while the wheels efficiently delivered suffering, authorities eventually recognized permanent damage outweighing any redemption. So Britain banned treadwheel use by 1898 for extreme cruelty. Yet little did Cubitt or authorities know that versions of his instrument would someday propel world fitness rather than punish prisoners.

From Punishing Hearts to Strengthening Them

As an urbanized 20th century ushered sedentary living, exercise gained new appeal for battling modern woes. Treadwheels conceptually reemerged as research tools gauging patient heart rates during motion. Modifying cattle treadmills in the 1940s, Seattle cardiologist Dr. Robert Bruce developed gentle walking tests revealing cardiac weakness through monitoring electrocardiogram (EKG) readouts. First used upholding astronaut fitness standards, the tests uncovered silent heart conditions and saved lives.

This promising diagnostic utility restored reputations for Cubitt's demonic invention. Exercise physiologist Dr. Kenneth Cooper next confirmed cardiorespiratory fitness strengthens the heart through his landmark 1968 book "Aerobics" advocating running.

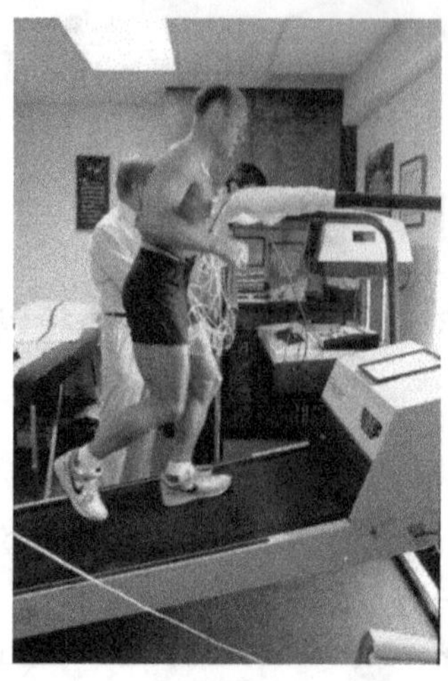

Clarence Bass Treadmill Cooper
Clinic by Justin Joseph 1989

Cooper's military research had employed treadmills quantifying exertion thresholds. Now enshrined as medical instruments and training aids, treadwheels seemed reformed from penal legacy. Yet drab decor still inspired bored misery users yearned escaping. An inventive New Jersey engineer named Bill Staub set sights on renovating that reputation next.

Bringing Treadmills Home

In the 1960s, few suburban homes housed exercise equipment beyond scattered dumbbells. Barred from running outdoors through harsh New Jersey winters, ex-jet engineer Bill Staub instead jury-rigged a motorized treadbelt from wooden rollers in his basement. Mimicking walking by adjusting the speed dial, early "treadmill prototypes let Staub train year-round chasing fitness milestones promoted by exercise guru Cooper without leaving home.

Sensing dilettante interest, Staub launched production of his PaceMaster treadmill via mail order in 1968. Costing today's equivalent of $3,000, Staub's " Basement Jogger" became the first machine marketing cardio training to consumers. Rival brands materialized once Staub proved home treadmill demand. Marketers now promised treadwheel workouts fostering wellness rather than inmate torture.

Sales boomed through the 1970s running craze. But while 50 million Americans now tread yearly, critics echo convict laments given 30% gather dust swiftly post-purchase as novelty fades. Can we break torturous reputations beyond glossy infomercial depictions? Modern inventors keep working towards that transformation.

Pace Master 600 Brochure cover, 1968

Today's Treadmills

Given most loathe treadmills despite owning them, innovators try rescuing workouts from tedium through creative variety transforming drudgery into adventure. Some approaches add tornado simulation for sprinters, video classes led by coaches, or immersive video game worlds full of alien creatures and fantasy quests unfolding through miles traveled. Participants now train alongside fellow cyclist avatars chasing checkered flags or stride across Google's Street View chasing scenery from Machu Picchu to Grand Canyon trails.

The most captivating trend transforms treadmills into portals venturing anywhere on Earth without leaving home. NordicTrack's patented design revolutionized machinery constricted as flat motorized tracks by introducing adjustable inclines. Gradually sloping treadmills mimic real running courses down to descending mountain trails, not just upwards hiking. Hands-free controls automatically match video footage pace evacuating the sensation of marathon monotony.

Has NordicTrack perfected the treadwheel legacy besieged by torture complaints since Cubitt's primitive paddles? Early reviews praise the immersion sensation finally achieving inventor Staub's initial suburban convenience vision.

And improved exercise adherence makes the upgraded daily treadmill grind easier embracing than previous generations endured.

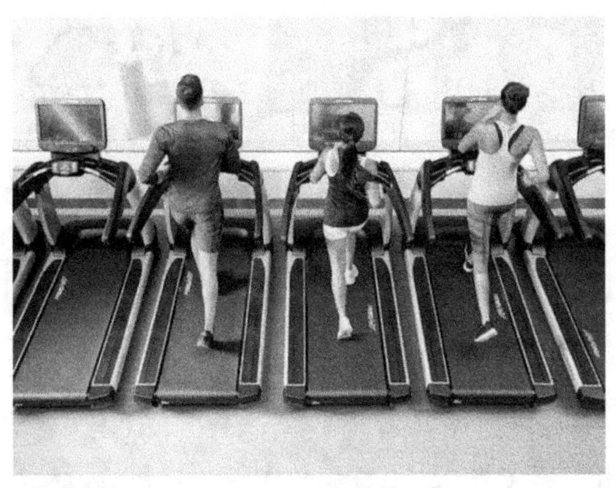

Reimagining Suffering

From British prisons to American basements towards global connectivity, treadmills symbolize cultural imagination's power redefining reviled objects through reenvisioning value. Had authorities banished Cubitt's torturous innovation outright back in 1898, cardio medicine and historic fitness revolutions may have unfolded very differently.

Instead, transformative minds redeemed the treadwheel's potential - migrating a mechanism of institutional suffering towards elevating health for all. Reform now spurs rehabilitation. What once inflicted humiliation offers personal power over the modern epidemics of obesity and heart disease. Stares of anxiety replaced by affirmation in the mirror.

There is poetic justice witnessed each day through throngs dynamically walking, running and climbing together in rhythm united by motivation versus restraint. Though fiberglass and silicon machinery updated materials, Cubitt might still recognize kindred spiraling momentum echoed from his 19th century lumber invention. Yet rather than crushing of convict spirit, devotees now reinforce persevering commitment to self-improvement first sparked by misfortune.

So while "dreadmills" remain logged by some, for others each step powers purpose strong enough overpowering adversity's lingering ghosts. Our shared progress was only possible reimagining anguish into inspiration when trapped fate seemed sealed. And the vista widens ahead wherever reclaiming pain for gain points progress next.

NIGHTCLUB BOUNCER WHO BECAME POPE

Before becoming the head of the Catholic Church in 2013, Pope Francis lived a much simpler life back in Argentina. In fact, he held an unusual job for a future pope - he worked as a bouncer at a nightclub.

Long before he was known as the "People's Pope," Jorge Bergoglio was a typical young man trying to support himself in Buenos Aires. He didn't grow up with much money and needed to work odd jobs to get by. Sticking to his humble roots, he labored as a bouncer, or doorman, at a local bar in the chaotic capital city.

photo of Jorge Mario Bergoglio as a young man

It may seem bizarre to imagine the future pontiff checking IDs and tossing unruly patrons out of a nightclub. But this down-to-earth experience likely helped shape his compassionate worldview. As pope, Francis became known for advocating on behalf of the poor and vulnerable.

His background differs drastically from recent popes who came from academic backgrounds. Pope Benedict XVI, for instance, was an esteemed theologian and professor in Germany before ascending to the papacy.

Bergoglio's life took a completely different path. He was born in 1936 to a working-class railroad family. To help make ends meet, he took menial jobs like sweeping floors and working in a chemical laboratory. These were the humble beginnings of a man who would become pope to over 1 billion Catholics worldwide.

Francis poses for a photo during an Easter procession in 2000.

Breaking 600 Years of Tradition

Francis made history when he became the first pope to resign from the papacy since 1415. Benedict XVI voluntarily stepped down in 2013, citing declining mental and physical health. He broke a tradition that popes serve until their death.

The unprecedented move set the stage for the conclave of cardinals to elect Cardinal Bergoglio as pope. At 76 years old, Francis was considered relatively old for a new pope. But he brought a renewed energy and more progressive vision to the church after replacing the scholarly Benedict.

Francis greets parishioners in Buenos Aires.

The People's Pope

From the start, Pope Francis diverged from Benedict's more formal and reserved style. He declined the luxurious papal apartment and private limousine, preferring a modest hotel room and public transportation. This aligns with his focus on serving the poor and leading the church with humility and simplicity.

Francis has championed refugees, pushed for action on climate change, and sought to make the church more welcoming to marginalized groups. His pastoral style aims to help everyday people connect with their faith.

While some traditional Catholics have criticized his progressive stances, he maintains widespread popularity, especially with young people drawn to his authenticity. For many, Francis exemplifies what a modern pope should be - a humble, caring leader in touch with ordinary folks.

It seems his past struggles and unassuming jobs helped shape that mindset. Francis learned early the meaning of hard work, empathy and service to the community - values that now define his papacy. The unexpected nightclub bouncer found his higher calling as the People's Pope.

Francis holds Mass outside a church in Buenos Aires in 2009.

WWI'S REMARKABLE CHRISTMAS TRUCE

Christmas Eve 1914 descended towards midnight under bone-chilling skies over Belgium's deadlocked Western Front. For British machine gunner Bruce Bairnsfather hunkering in muddy trenches with the Royal Warwickshires, thoughts drifted homeward across the growling guns. Rather than family comforts, his dreary shelters three feet deep offered only ceaseless combat's signature harvest - sleeplessness, hunger, infection, dismemberment, madness - with each day narrowly dodging death's next careless swing.

Yet suddenly tender strains of "Stille Nacht" floated through the darkness from German lines mere hundreds of yards away. Then the British picked up the cues, voices rising together with "Silent Night's" familiar English refrains. Just months ago most believed the war would end by Christmas, Bairnsfather mused. Could carols finally herald truce from this horrific entanglement? Incredibly before dawn, a bizarre armistice unfurled as if heaven-sent to hell.

Troops Gingerly Venture Forth On Christmas Morn

When opposing trenches both fell silent, the British grew suspicious. Then, accented English shouts rang out: "Come over here!" Sergeant Stanley Holmes bravely answered: "You come halfway, we come halfway." Thus did the inconceivable occur in ultimate No Man's land: sworn killing machines strolling out, unarmed, to make nice.

"Eventually a German said, 'Tomorrow you no shoot, we no shoot,'" British rifleman J. Reading later penned home. "They were Saxons and one fellow talked English!" gasped amazed infantryman Archibald Stanley. "Cor blimey mate...I was in a London hotel when the war broke out!". It turned out peaceful gestures needn't trump bitter hatreds or strict orders against fraternity. Contingents along the front observed impromptu goodwill and rest while remaining units gladly carried on hostilities.

A snapshot taken by a British officer showing German and British troops fraternising on the Western Front during the Christmas Truce of 1914.

Yet where generosity emerged that Christmas, shared humanity enticed men to suspend their commissioned savagery without an official truce. "You couldn't have got such a quiet sector," marvelled Sergeant George Beckwith. "It was just like a moonlit night at home, with a bit of snow on the ground." Such fleeting tranquility, however relative, surely proved a welcomed reprieve.

Foes Bury Dead, Swap Treats, And Sport Across Divide

In the barbed wasteland between French and German trenches, incredulous Lieutenant Kurt Zehmisch described British Tommies hoisting a soccer ball aloft in the crisp afternoon. Impromptu goals took shape, ushering in raucous match between recent bombardment targets. To civilian outsiders it appeared a cordial game with lives at stake after ceasefire's end. Yet to frozen conscripts trudging the same few scarred yards and witnessing horrific mortality for interminable months, surely any playful sleeves felt divine.

Less vigorous interludes reigned across many miles that landmark holiday as enemies gathered to perform grim rites or simple communion. "What do you know, the Jerries are out on top; they're walking about, they're dishing out drinks and cigarettes!" whooped, overjoyed British cavalrymen George Jameson and Philip Ridley, proudly sporting German caps and canteens upon return to camp. Others joined solemn processions with candles or lantern light flickering in the profound darkness. Fading notes of "Stille Nacht" echoed again as former killers together gently lowered the frozen dead into Belgium's ever-welcoming earth.

Some recounted years after families struggling for closure finally learned fates of husbands,

Soldiers playing soccer in No-Man's Land
during the Christmas Truce in 1914.

fathers, sons expired anonymously on battlefields suddenly bridged by compassion. "You know, we couldn't have gone on in the First Battle of Ypres because you had so many reserves in your woods," London fusilier Henry Williamson informed a German officer, mutually affirming the survivors' burdens. Where truce emerged, ravenous fighters who hadn't properly slept or eaten in weeks found sustaining crumbs of mutual respect.

High Command Orders End To "Deplorable" Peace

Yet romance fades quicker than despair for those tasked with managing violence. Once discovered by the high brass, fury rained down by telephone and telegraph. "Get back in your trenches every man!" echoed outraged voices of generals safe behind Belgian lines. Bewildered Tommies shaking Saxons' hands one minute were threatened as deserters the next.

"Course that started the war again. Ooh we were cursing them to hell, cursing the generals and that," fumed lance corporal George Ashurst at orders to fire upon their peacemaking comrades of hours before. However dynamically compassion seized the lower ranks that remarkable Yuletide, top brass proved unwilling to entertain potential cracks in martial order. By necessity soldiers are trained as ruthlessly obedient actors, not autonomous souls.

So this brief nourishing glow between men born innocents but transformed into enemies flickered out under stern repression. No further Christmas Truces would grace the Western Front's remainder as the upper echelon clamped down. Yet wheregunners mowed lines and sowed screams anew, tender sprigs of reconciliation took lasting root in some hearts.

The Truce Becomes Legendary Over Decades

High command resolved to contain further unofficial outbreaks of fellowship along the front. Still, news of peculiar 1914 holiday meetings gradually reached public circles. Soldiers' letters revealing soccer kickabouts and joint burials between trenches were published openly by January 1915 without apparent repercussions. By war's end the Truce became artistic inspiration across literature and music expressing deeply held yearning for unity.

Though impossible to verify precise scale, the Great War's fleeting peace at least briefly converted stretches totaling many miles into temporary demilitarized zones. Estimates claim over 100,000 among millions of embattled troops participated in various displays of what unveiled as underlying brotherhood between Europeans slaughtering each other by the tens of thousands.

The Football Remembers Memorial at the National Memorial Arboretum in England, commemorating the 1914 Christmas Truce.

Far from hiding this profoundly inspiring event, the Truce earned global renown. Paintings, sculptures, advertisements, television and Hollywood films ensued over the century. In 2014 the English and German soccer teams movingly competed in friendly match during a memorial centenary gathering. And England's National Memorial Arboretum features the prominent "Football Remembers" sculpture commemorating impromptu kickabouts in No Man's Land that Christmas.

British and German officers meeting in No-Man's Land during the unofficial truce.

Enduring Takeaways

Looking back across the unfathomable man-made calamity unfolding daily along shell-blasted Belgium plains, the suddenly suspended carnage of Christmas 1914 almost strains credulity. Yet theImpromptu goodwill exchanges and cessations undeniably occurred without formal decree. No less astounding, the original belligerent inspiration was merely hearing songs of the Savior's purported "peace on earth towards men of good will" arising from enemies' frigid outposts.

What profound truths lie cradled in this war story for the ages? Men young and worldly, patriotic and dutiful, faced the same holiday tugs of compassion towards fellows suffering senselessly as themselves. We can glean from numerous accounts that only ignorance bred through distances physical and cultural perhaps enabled propaganda convincing millionsto crave killing one another. And we can conclude from brigadier blowback that even intensely bonded killing comrades threaten rigid tribal hierarchy.

But more universally, the improbable Christmas Truce speaks to transcendent human yearnings for tranquility and belonging beyond caste, customs, banners, geopolitics. Its legend survived and inspired because, for a fleeting thin slice of eternity, simple soldier empathy plainly revealed war's great lie: concocted enmity to leverage human sacrifice on vast scale indeed demands consistent emotional suppression.

What "treasonous" truce occurred was not an organized rebellion but organic surging of spirit no disciplinary threat could forever quell. Its persistence in legend reminds us that, however obscured behind draped flags and horns, the deepest human essence seeks connection and community with all. And if we LET true good will take flesh, exceptional miracles like a soccer ball briefly replacing bullets might surprise us all one silent night.

THE MOST DANGEROUS MOVIE EVER FILMED

In the annals of cinematic history, few films have earned the dubious distinction of being labeled "the most dangerous movie ever made." But one film stands out for its sheer audacity and the unbelievable risks taken by its cast and crew which included Tippi Hedren as the star. The film called Roar the Movie. A 1981 adventure film produced by Tippi Hedren's husband, Noel Marshall. This is the story of how a Hollywood couple's dream project turned into a nightmare of epic proportions. It forever changed the lives of those involved and leaving an indelible mark on the world of filmmaking.

It all began in 1969 when Tippi Hedren and Noel Marshall embarked on a safari vacation in Tanzania. Enthralled by the majestic lions they encountered, the couple was struck by the idea of making a film. They wanted to showcase these magnificent creatures. They wanted to raise awareness about their plight in the face of human encroachment. The Marshalls envisioned a groundbreaking production that would capture the raw beauty and power of the big cats. They also wanted to deliver a compelling narrative that would captivate audiences worldwide.

Little did they know that their noble intentions would lead them down a path fraught with danger, chaos, and unimaginable challenges. The couple's determination to bring their vision to life would be tested at every turn. They navigated the treacherous waters of an unconventional film production that defied all industry norms and safety standards.

Noel and Tippi with a lion

Bringing the Vision to Life

Determined to bring their vision Roar the movie to the screen, Tippi Hedren and Noel Marshall soon realized that traditional Hollywood methods wouldn't suffice. No animal trainers were willing to provide the number of lions required for the film. The scenes demanded unprecedented close interaction between the big cats and human actors. The risks were simply too high, and the liability too great.

Noel on the set of 'Roar'

Undeterred by the obstacles in their path, the couple made a fateful decision. They would import and breed their own pride of lions. It was a bold and unprecedented move. One that would require immense resources, dedication, and a willingness to put themselves and their family in harm's way.

The Marshall estate quickly became home to a growing number of cubs, which delighted the family at first. The playful young lions frolicking on the grounds of their property made Tippi Hedren and Noel Marshall's dream come true. They saw in them the promise of a revolutionary film. One that would change the way the world viewed these majestic creatures.

Spiraling out of Control

However, as the lions matured into unruly adolescents, the situation spiraled out of control. The once-adorable cubs grew into powerful, unpredictable predators. The Marshalls found themselves struggling to maintain control over their burgeoning pride. Neighbors complained about the roars and growls emanating from the property. The couple soon realized that they needed to find a more suitable home for their "babies."

Undaunted, Noel Marshall invested a significant portion of the couple's fortune into constructing a sprawling ranch. This ranch would serve as both a sanctuary for the lions and a film set for their ambitious production. The ranch, located in the heart of California, was a marvel of engineering and design. It featured vast enclosures and sound stages. It also had a full-scale replica of a colonial mansion. The mansion would serve as the backdrop for the film's climactic scenes.

Chaos on the Set

With the stage set for Roar the movie, their grand production, Hedren and Marshall eagerly welcomed a menagerie of wild animals. This included lions, tigers, and cheetahs, onto their California property. The air was electric with anticipation as the couple prepared to embark on the most ambitious and dangerous film shoot of their careers.

Tippi in 'Roar'

But as filming began, it became apparent that the untrained beasts had no intention of following a script. The set devolved into a chaotic and unpredictable environment, with the animals asserting their dominance at every turn. The cast and crew had no prior experience working with wild animals. Yet, they found themselves at the mercy of the big cats. These animals seemed to view them as little more than playthings or potential prey

The unruly animals quickly mauled, bit, and scratched the actors and crew members, causing injuries to mount rapidly. Noel Marshall himself nearly lost his life to an infection after being attacked by one of the lions. This incident forced the production to halt temporarily as he recovered from his wounds.

Remaining Determined

Despite the growing toll of injuries and the escalating danger on set, Tippi Hedren and Noel Marshall remained determined to see their vision through to the end. They pressed on, even as the financial burden of the project grew increasingly heavy. The emotional strain also began to take its toll on their relationship and their family.

The couple's daughter, Melanie Griffith, had also been recruited to star in the film alongside her mother. She eventually found herself at the center of some of the most harrowing scenes. She was at one point, mauled by a lion and required extensive facial reconstructions to repair the damage. The incident left her deeply traumatized. It also strained her relationship with her mother, who she felt had prioritized the film over her safety and well-being.

As the production dragged on, the set became a pressure cooker of tension and fear. The cast and crew lived in constant terror of the next attack.

No one knew when one of the big cats might lash out or turn on them. The way to describe the atmosphere was one of barely contained chaos. The line between reality and fiction blurring as the animals exerted their will over the hapless humans who had dared to invade their domain.

Tippi Hedren in her home with one of her rescued animals at the Shambala Preserve, Acton, California, 1982

Blood and Redemption

After nearly six years of filming, Roar the movie finally wrapped, leaving a trail of over 70 injuries in its wake. The finished product, while undeniably spectacular in its raw depiction of human-animal interaction, was a box office failure. It ended up grossing a mere $2 million against its $17 million budget.

However, the film's troubled production did manage to raise awareness about the plight of big cats and the importance of conservation efforts.

Tippi Hedren and Noel Marshall's misguided attempt to showcase the majesty of these creatures had inadvertently shone a light on the dangers of keeping wild animals in captivity. It also showed the need for greater protections for these magnificent beasts.

Passion into The Preserve

For Tippi Hedren, the experience left an indelible mark. She channeled her passion and her guilt into founding the Shambala Preserve. The preserve was a sanctuary for big cats that had been exploited by the entertainment industry. Through this endeavor, she found a measure of redemption and purpose in the wake of Roar's tumultuous journey.

Hedren transformed the preserve into a haven for dozens of lions, tigers, and other big cats after their former owners had abandoned or mistreated them. She dedicated herself to providing these animals with a safe and nurturing environment. These cats could live out their lives in peace and dignity.

The Making of a Cult Classic

Despite its initial failure, Roar the movie has since gained a cult following. Audiences marvel at the sheer audacity of the filmmakers and the incredible footage captured on screen.

The film stands as a testament to the lengths some will go to pursue their dreams. It's a testament to perseverance even in the face of overwhelming adversity and danger.

For many, Roar represents a bygone era of filmmaking, when the boundaries between reality and fiction were blurred, and the line between bravery and foolishness was often crossed in the name of art. The film's legacy has only grown in the decades since its release, with new generations of cinephiles discovering its strange and captivating power.

A Cautionary Tale of Hubris

In the end, Roar serves as a cautionary tale about the perils of hubris and the unpredictability of nature. It is a reminder that even the noblest of intentions can lead us down a treacherous path, and that sometimes, the greatest triumphs are born from the ashes of our most catastrophic failures.

Big cat fever consumed every aspect of Hedren's life and she regrets how it might have affected the relationship with her daughter: 'Many times over the subsequent years, I've wondered if Melanie felt I'd devoted so much attention to the big cats we were amassing that there wasn't enough left for her'

The story of Roar is one of passion, perseverance, and ultimately, redemption. It is a tale of two Hollywood dreamers who dared to pursue their vision, no matter the cost, and who emerged from the crucible of their own creation forever changed.

Their legacy, like the film itself, is one of both tragedy and triumph, a testament to the enduring power of the human spirit in the face of unimaginable adversity.

As we look back on the making of Roar, we are reminded of the thin line that separates our dreams from our nightmares, and the courage it takes to walk that line in pursuit of something greater than ourselves. It is a story that will continue to inspire and caution us in equal measure, a reminder of the beauty and the danger that lurks at the heart of the natural world, and the lengths we will go to capture it on film.

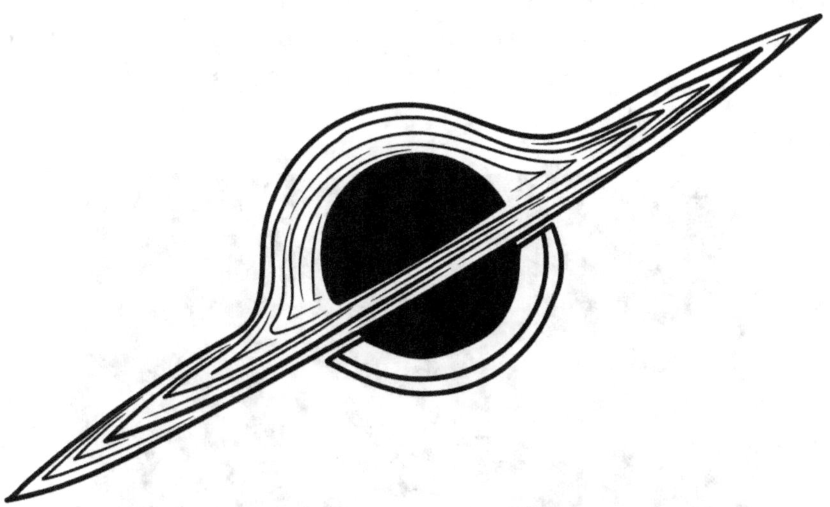

THE DARKEST AND THE BRIGHTEST OBJECT IN THE UNIVERSE IS THE SAME

In the vast expanse of our cosmic playground, Black Holes reign supreme as enigmatic wonders. They simultaneously perplex and captivate astronomers and space lovers alike. As the darkest and brightest objects in the universe, they present an enthralling paradox. It invites us to explore their mysteries further.

From Earth, the brightest object in our sky is undoubtedly the Sun. It's a star so close to us that it outshines all others during the day. When night falls, we can observe stars of varying brightness, something astronomers have been doing for millennia.

Luminosity and Distance

Over 2,000 years ago, Greek astronomer Hipparchus devised a classification system for stars based on their apparent or visual magnitude. However the brightness of the stars we see in the sky can deceive us to their true brilliance. In reality, stars that seem equally bright might differ in luminosity due to their distance from us. A closer fainter star may seem brighter than a star that is 10,000 times more bright but is 100,000 times farther away. To overcome this limitation, astronomers developed an absolute magnitude scale to determine an objects' true luminosity.

Black Holes: Darkest Cosmic Objects

Now, picture a corner of space so unimaginably dark that not even the fastest thing in the universe, light, can't break free—say hello to Black Holes! These celestial enigmas are born from the remnants of massive stars that have collapsed under their own crushing gravity. Their event horizon, or the point of no return, marks a boundary where everything that crosses its threshold is gobbled up, leaving no trace behind. This feature crowns black holes as the darkest objects in our cosmic realm.

Quasars: Outshining an Entire Galaxy

However, as Neil DeGrasse Tyson once pointed out, "the Universe has no obligation to make sense to you." In spite of their innate darkness, Black Holes can indirectly create some of the most spectacular light displays in the Universe. As a black hole's gravity draws in nearby matter, the material spirals around the event horizon in a disk-like formation. The friction between particles generates enormous amounts of heat, ultimately producing intense light and radiation. In some cases, this radiant spectacle can even outshine entire galaxies!

Enter Quasars, the most luminous objects in the universe. These celestial beacons are powered by supermassive black holes at the core of galaxies, and they emit light of such staggering intensity that it rivals the combined brightness of countless suns. Despite their immense distance from Earth, quasars can be observed, thanks to their extraordinary brilliance.

But black holes don't stop there! They also give birth to other fascinating phenomena like active galactic nuclei (AGNs) and X-ray binaries. Though smaller and less luminous than quasars, AGNs still produce incredible light displays as they devour matter from their host galaxies. X-ray binaries, on the other hand, consist of a black hole orbiting a regular star, emitting powerful X-ray radiation that makes them some of the most radiant X-ray sources in the sky.

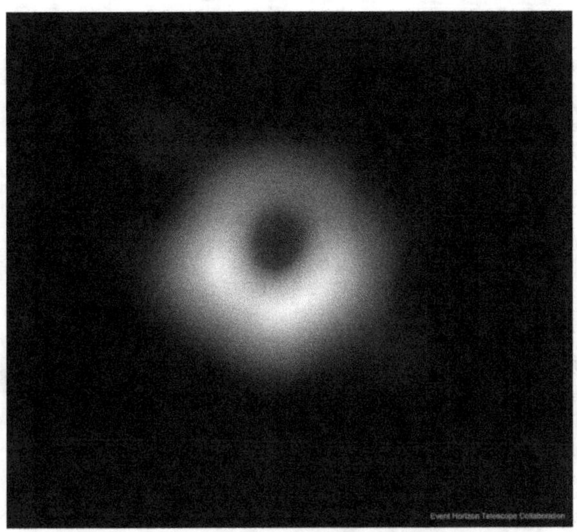

Actual picture of a Super Massive black hole at the center of M87 galaxy.
The black portion is the shadow of the Black Hole and can
fit our entire solar system inside

The Paradox of Black Holes

The paradox of black holes being both the darkest and brightest objects in the universe underscores the intricate and awe-inspiring nature of our cosmos. It serves as a gentle reminder that there are still many mysteries waiting to be unraveled within the universe's vast expanse.

As we continue to investigate black holes and uncover more of their enigmatic secrets, we not only expand our understanding of the universe but also marvel at the fascinating cosmic riddle that these shadowy yet luminous wonders encapsulate.

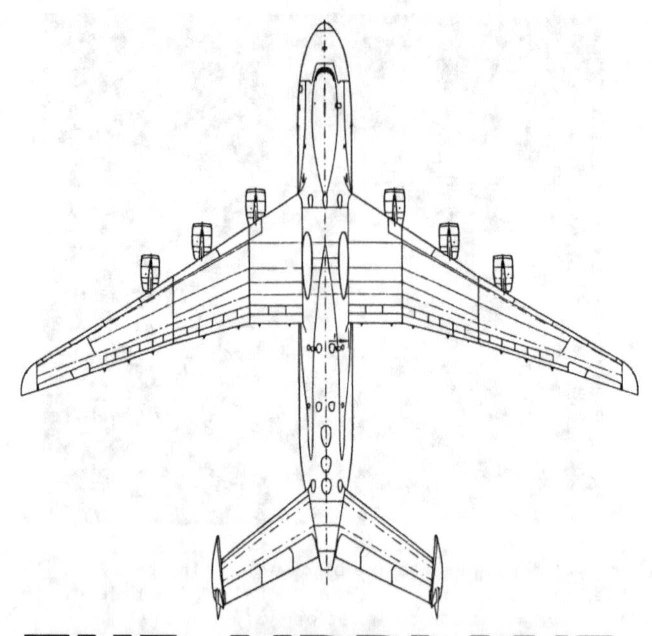

THE AIRPLANE GRAVEYARD

In the Arizona desert near Tucson sprawls a one-of-a-kind retirement community - but it's not for retirees. It's for historic military aircraft that have flown their final missions. This aviation "elephant's graveyard" is called the 309th Aerospace Maintenance and Regeneration Group, or AMARG.

Over 4,400 retired planes from the Air Force, Navy, Marines, Army, Coast Guard, and NASA reside here in the dry Southwest climate. As the largest airplane boneyard in the world, AMARG provides critical long-term storage, maintenance, and parts reclamation for the nation's excess military fleet.

From Post-War Origins to Modern Operations

AMARG's origins trace back to immediately after World War II. With massive surpluses of aircraft after winning the war, the Army Air Forces urgently needed storage space. Davis-Monthan Air Force Base near Tucson was selected as an ideal spot thanks to its arid desert climate, alkaline soil, and minimal corrosion issues.

In 1946, the base rapidly filled up with over 600 B-29 Superfortress bombers and 200 C-47 Skytrain transports. Some were later reactivated for the Korean War, while many others were scrapped for parts or sold off. This set the precedent for an ongoing aircraft boneyard at Davis-Monthan's sprawling facilities.

Throughout the Cold War era, the base's plane storage operations continued expanding to consolidate obsolete models from all military branches. As new generations of jets and helicopters replaced propeller-driven aircraft, the boneyard provided an economical way to house the excess airfleet.

Today, with about 550 employees, AMARG manages a staggering inventory of historic and modern aircraft. Its workload includes reclaiming parts, supporting museum displays, and converting planes to target drones.

Ariel view of Davis-Monthan Air Force Base

Ideal Conditions in the Desert

Hot, arid Arizona makes a perfect environment for storing aircraft in the long term. The low humidity and dry desert climate minimize corrosion issues that can plague planes in other environments.

With just 11 inches of rainfall annually, costly concrete ramps aren't necessary either - planes can simply be towed around on the hard, alkaline soil without sinking or getting stuck. The lack of precipitation also reduces problems with rust and frost damage.

While Arizona's abundance of sunshine necessitates careful sealing of the aircraft from heat, dust and sunlight, the Southwest climate still offers ideal overall conditions for preserving mothballed planes indefinitely.

Massive Inventory and Meticulous Maintenance

The AMARG facility encompasses a sprawling 2,600 acres - about 4 square miles. The retired aircraft are neatly lined up in rows and formations on the compacted desert soil, contrasting with typical crowded flight line parking.

Various aircraft lined up at AMARG

The inventory includes historic planes such as WWII-era B-29 Superfortresses and B-52 Stratofortresses from the Cold War era. Iconic fighter jets like F-4 Phantoms, F-14 Tomcats, and F-16 Fighting Falcons are also well represented.

While some aircraft are kept in near flight-ready condition, others are designated for reclamation of parts. Technicians continually assess and preserve select planes based on their storage status and needs.

In addition to military warplanes, the AMARG boneyard contains rare prototypes, trainers, test aircraft, and even NASA's remaining space shuttles pre-museum delivery.

Visiting the Legendary Boneyard

As an active military base, public access to Davis-Monthan and the AMARG tour requires advanced planning and restrictions. Guests must have ID and U.S. citizenship or prior approval to enter the base.

But for aviation buffs, the extra logistics are worth it. The 2-3 hour bus tour provides a unique up-close view of famous planes like the B-52 bomber and F-14 Tomcat fighter. Visitors can also spot aircraft from the Air Force, Navy, Marines, Army, Coast Guard, and NASA.

Walking the grounds, one can't help but feel the ghosts of aviation history all around. The neatly lined aircraft stand as testaments to engineering ingenuity and the pilots who brought them to life. Their faded squadron insignia hint at stories waiting to be retold.

For over 75 years now, this Arizona aircraft boneyard has allowed the Armed Forces to economically store its retired fleet in ideal conditions. Carefully preserved, these dormant planes seem to echo with memories of their glory days soaring aloft.

SMOKING WEED AT THE WHITE HOUSE

In September 1980, country music legend Willie Nelson found himself in one of the most coveted smoke spots imaginable - the White House roof. During a stay at the presidential residence, Nelson and a companion stealthily made their way to the rooftop overlooking DC for a discreet joint. This audacious toking session entered Nelson lore, with the mystery companion's identity only recently confirmed as none other than Chip Carter, Jimmy Carter's son.

Willie Nelson's Well-Known Pot Love

Willie Nelson is about as legendary for his love of weed as he is for his music. The outlaw country pioneer has built his image around being America's most beloved stoner uncle. So it's not shocking he'd be down to burn one in the White House if the chance arose.

Nelson has openly touted the benefits of marijuana for decades. In his songs, interviews, and memoirs, he's extolled the virtues of lighting up. And he's become an endearing advocate for cannabis legalization.

Country Music Legends Willie Nelson and
Emmylou Harris Visit President Jimmy Carter
in the Oval Office, 1980

So when Nelson scored an overnight stay at 1600 Pennsylvania Avenue in 1980, he couldn't pass up the opportunity for a White House smoke session. At the time, Nelson was at the height of his pot-loving notoriety, having been arrested just a year earlier in Texas for possession. Clearly, a little thing like being in the president's home wasn't going to stop Nelson from enjoying some herb.

A Late Night Roof Adventure

The opportunity presented itself in 1980, when Nelson performed at the White House and stayed overnight as a guest of President Jimmy Carter. Nelson wrote in his 1988 memoir that late into the evening, a "White House insider" offered him a private tour ending on the roof, where the two casually lit up beneath the stars.

Though Nelson coyly kept his smoking buddy anonymous, many speculated it was Chip Carter, the president's adventurous middle son. But Nelson remained tight-lipped, and the ceiling-high session became woven into his eccentric life lore.

For decades, the tale seemed more apt for Nelson's elaborately mythic persona than actual reality. But the truth has gradually come out.

Confirmation from the Source

In the 2020 documentary Jimmy Carter: Rock & Roll President, the peanut farmer-turned-president himself spilled the secret - yes, it was his own son Nelson smoked with.

"He says it was one of the servants at the White House," said a chuckling Carter. "Actually, it was one of my sons."

Chip Carter subsequently confirmed it, recalling how after Nelson's show, he suggested going up to the roof to take in the view. Nelson told Chip, "Let's go upstairs" until they reached the top with a joint in hand.

For Nelson's part, he's expressed not wanting to out Chip as a "pot-smoker like him." But now the truth is out - Willie Nelson smoked weed with the president's son on the White House roof.

Jimmy Carter and his wife Rosalynn Carter on stage with Willie Nelson

The Aftermath

Remarkably, Nelson's overnight stay and pot use didn't spark any presidential fury or consequences. While Carter's Baptist roots made him no fan of drug use, he maintained an amiable friendship with Nelson despite their differences.

Carter tolerated Nelson's marijuana lifestyle, recognizing his immense talent and cultural significance. And Nelson returned the respect, calling Carter "a great president" in his memoir. Their unlikely bond thrived despite clashing outlooks.

2020 documentary Jimmy Carter: Rock & Roll President

But the White House weed caper remained hidden until after Carter left office. Nelson first went public about it in his memoir after Reagan took over. By then, any fallout was no longer Carter's concern.

While the illicit roof rip understandably stayed hush-hush, its reveal decades later only bolsters Nelson's legendary status. It represents the ultimate clash of the outlaw country stalwart and the buttoned-up presidency.

That night, Nelson not only lit up a bone, but also briefly lit up the often pretentious White House atmosphere. He brought the irreverent spirit of the anti-establishment decade into the halls of ultimate power and propriety.

Life long friendship

Final Thoughts

Over 40 years later, Nelson remains a cannabis advocate, having launched his own marijuana brand Willie's Reserve. Meanwhile, the White House remains federal land where pot possession gets you handcuffed, whether you're a guest or president's kid.

But for one night in 1980, Nelson and Chip Carter pulled off a bold law-breaking feat. Their discrete yet daring rooftop smoke session now enters White House lore as an amusing moment when cannabis infiltrated the highest office.

While presidents since Carter have become progressively more marijuana-friendly, the plant is still forbidden at the White House. Nelson and Carter's ceiling rip is a reminder of the cultural gap that can exist between stodgy politicians and unconventional musicians. But for one night, herb brought them together at the pinnacle of power.

THE SWARM THAT BLOCKED THE SUN FOR DAYS

In the summer of 1874, a specter began to loom over the Great Plains, from North Dakota all the way down to Texas. This was no ordinary threat, but a living, swarming, voracious one. It came in the form of billions of Rocky Mountain locusts, whose sheer numbers filled the sky, obscuring the sun for five incredible days.

Post-Civil War settlers, having relocated to this vast expanse for a chance at a better life, were about to be confronted with an unprecedented calamity. The abundant rains of spring had held the promise of a bountiful harvest, only for the summer to be seized by drought - a condition not just unfortunate for the farmers but the perfect setup for the incoming horde of locusts.

This locust swarm was part of a familiar life cycle. Normally, at low population densities, these insects behave like their close relatives, the grasshoppers. However, when crowded, a chemical transformation begins, triggered by cues from their feces and disturbance of tiny hairs on their hind legs. It's an astonishing metamorphosis turning an ordinary insect into a voracious mob.

A Locust Storm Descends

The Rocky Mountain locust, naturally native to drier habitats, found the arid conditions conducive and took flight in search of sustenance. These insects, typically about an inch and a half in length, descended upon the prairies in late July. They had journeyed from the mountains of Colorado, Wyoming, and Montana, and they seemed unending.

The locusts, as reported by an awestruck farmer, looked "like a great white cloud, like a snowstorm, blocking out the sun like vapor." Their arrival was sudden and overwhelming.

Farmers rushed to shield their crops and wells, a futile gesture against the unyielding locusts who munched through even fabric coverings.

It was the largest congregation of animal life ever recorded by humans; a super-organism composed of an estimated 120 billion to 12.5 Trillion individuals. A metabolic wildfire racing across the Great Plains, decimating a vast region of pioneer agriculture and leaving devastation in its wake.

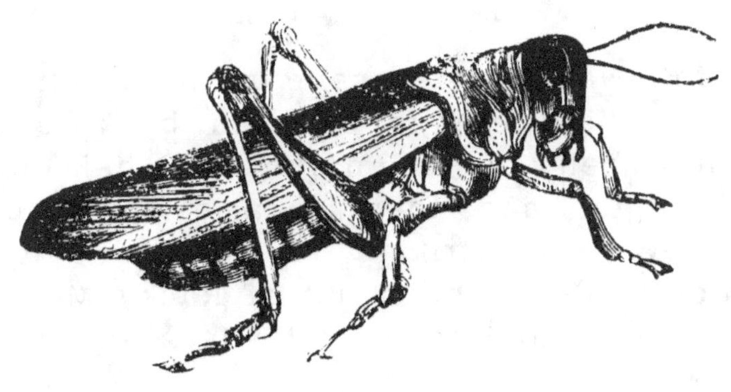

Imagine a swarm so enormous, it covered an estimated area of 198,000 square miles - nearly the combined size of the states of Wyoming and Colorado. In the "Second Report of the United States Entomological Commission," Dr. A.L. Child of the U.S. Signal Corps calculated these staggering figures by clocking the insects' speed and telegraphing surrounding towns. The locusts streamed overhead, a suffocating mass of insects blotting out the sky for an unbelievable five days.

A field ravaged by locusts

What followed was a scene straight out of a horror movie, perhaps directed by Hitchcock himself. Their bodies darkened, their wings grew longer, and they became a rapacious swarm. With a striking resemblance to the "Mongol hordes," the cloud of Rocky Mountain locusts descended upon the landscape.

Laura Ingalls Wilder in her book "On the Banks of Plum Creek" depicted the surreal scene vividly. She recounted how the locusts, appearing like a dark cloud, began to rain down on the land. They covered every surface, clinging to the skin and clothes, their rasping wings filling the air with an eerie whirring sound. Their mass was so immense that the ground itself was concealed beneath a writhing layer of insects.

No Green Thing Safe

The locusts did not discriminate. After decimating the crops, they moved on to consuming wool straight from the sheep, clothing off people's backs, paper, tree bark, sawdust, leather, and even wooden tool handles. They left in their wake, a landscape stripped bare, as if ravaged by fire.

Those affected the most were the newcomers, the emigrants of western Kansas. As the insects covered the ground several inches deep, the steel tracks of the locomotives became too slick with their crushed bodies for trains to gain traction. One correspondent from the New York Times commented on the onslaught, noting that the locusts "beat against the houses, swarm in at the windows, cover the passing trains… They work as if sent to destroy."

Art depicting the Locust Plague of 1875

Locust swarm Wyoming, 1875

A Struggle for Survival

Amid the devastation, a grim reality took hold. Many couldn't survive, succumbing to starvation, as described heartbreakingly by a St. Louis Republican report that seemed to promise more graves marked "STARVED TO DEATH." To prevent such a dire situation, Governor Thomas A. Osborn called a special legislative session in September 1874. In response, the legislature approved $73,000 in bonds to aid the ravaged districts.

Such was the extent of the devastation that U.S. troops had to be mobilized to distribute food, blankets, and clothing to devastated farm families. The Rocky Mountain locusts had feasted on vegetation leaving the pioneers helpless in the face of their destructive appetite.

A plea for help echoed across America. The country responded, with supplies of beans, pork, rice, and seed transported free of charge by the railroads to the farmers in Kansas. The total assistance amounted to $235,108.47, along with clothing for more than 34,000 individuals.

Map of North America, illustrating the country east of the Rocky Mountains, overrun in 1874 by the Rocky Mountain Locust.
Prepared by C. V. Riley

The End of the Locust Plague

For three long years, the locusts held sway. Their devastation totaled $200 million in crop damage across several states, covering an area equivalent to California. Then, just as suddenly as it had begun, the Rocky Mountain locust began to mysteriously disappear in the late 1880s.

Farmers fighting the Locust swarm

One prevailing theory credits the settlers' agricultural practices for the locusts' eventual demise. The incessant plowing, irrigation, and trampling by cattle near rivers and streams in the Rocky Mountains might have destroyed their eggs in the areas they permanently inhabited. As a result, the once great swarm that blocked the sun for five days vanished from the earth. The last sighting of a Rocky Mountain locust was in 1902.

This tale serves as a vivid reminder of the resilience of the human spirit and our ability to adapt and survive in the face of even the most daunting of natural adversities. As we go about our lives in the quietude of the Great Plains today, let us remember the settlers of the past who stood their ground against the sky-darkening swarm of yesteryear.

STEPHEN HAWKING'S PARTY FOR TIME TRAVELERS

Back in 2009, the ever-curious and fun-loving physicist Stephen Hawking decided to throw a one-of-a-kind bash at the University of Cambridge. This wasn't your ordinary party; it was designed especially for time travelers.

Hawking's playful experiment not only showcased his creative side but also gave everyone a chance to think about the possibilities and challenges of time travel.

Imagine receiving an invitation that says, "You are cordially invited to a reception for Time Travellers." Sounds like a blast, right? Well, Hawking had a cheeky trick up his sleeve: he revealed the invitation on his TV show, "Into the Universe with Stephen Hawking," after the party had ended. The idea was that the invite would be around for ages and eventually reach a time where time travel was possible and a time traveler would pop back to join the festivities.

Invitation for Stephen Hawking's party for time travelers

During the show, Hawking eagerly awaited his guests, even joking about a "future Miss Universe" making a grand entrance. But as it turned out, no time travelers came to his shindig. The champagne went unopened, and the dance floor remained empty.

While it's a bummer that no time travelers showed up, their absence raises some interesting questions. Is time travel impossible, or is there another reason for the no-shows? In a later interview, Hawking mentioned that time travel might actually wreck "space-time itself". If that's the case, it's probably a good thing that no one RSVP'd "yes" to his time-traveling soiree.

Hawking's experiment serves as a fun reminder of the complexities of time travel. Even if it were possible, it might come with some serious risks. No time travelers attending his party could mean that future humans have realized the dangers and decided not to mess with the space-time continuum.

Stephen Hawking's 71st Birthday Party where his guests did show up

Beyond the science, Hawking's time traveler party is a testament to his playful personality and love for life. He didn't let physical challenges hold him back from exploring the universe or having a good time. This lighthearted experiment highlights not only his brilliant mind but also his ability to make complex ideas engaging and enjoyable for everyone.

So, Stephen Hawking's party for time travelers was a super fun way to explore the enigma of time travel and show off the imaginative side of a world-class physicist. Even though the future folks didn't make an appearance, the experiment still stands as a reminder of Hawking's creative spirit and passion for understanding the unknown. As we keep contemplating the mysteries of time travel and the cosmos, the incredible legacy of Stephen Hawking's adventurous spirit will continue to inspire generations of thinkers and party-goers alike.

Photo by Platon

SHE FELL OUT OF AN AIRPLANE AND LIVED

When Juliane Koepcke boarded LANSA Flight 508 on Christmas Eve in 1971, she was a carefree 17-year-old in a sleeveless dress and sandals. Aboard LANSA Flight 508, filled with holiday passengers all eager to reach their destinations, Juliane was blissfully unaware of the impending catastrophe that was about to unfold.

The plane, soaring through the stormy night skies, was unexpectedly struck by a fierce bolt of lightning. With a jolt that sent shockwaves through the hearts of everyone onboard, the plane began to plummet, descending rapidly into the unforgiving expanse of the Peruvian Amazon rainforest.

The thunderstorm had separated the row of seats Juliane was harnessed in. She remembered seeing the dense Peruvian rainforest 3,000 meters below and she plummeted towards the ground. She lost consciousness and assumed that her view of the rainforest may be her last.

"I was outside, in the open air. I hadn't left the plane; the plane had left me." Juliane later recalled in an interview.

She woke up with just a broken collarbone and a deep gash on her arm, somehow surviving a 3km fall. Out of the 92 souls onboard that doomed flight, only one emerged from the wreckage — young Juliane.

Defying the odds, she found herself alive, yet surrounded by an unfathomable tragedy. With the weight of a broken collarbone and a deep, ominous gash on her arm, she found herself on the threshold of an unimaginable challenge: a brutal journey through the unforgiving Amazon jungle, an alien world fraught with danger at every turn.

5 year old Juliane Koepcke with a White-throated Toucan (1959)

SURVIVING The Amazon

The crash had not only left her stranded in the merciless wilderness, but it had also thrust upon her a deeply painful realization: her mother, who was seated next to her just moments before the crash, was now nowhere to be found.

She remembered her mother's eerily calm last words just after Juliane had seen a flash of white light over the plane's wing causing the plane to nose dive: "Now it's all over."

She was forced to grapple with the harsh truth that her mother was gone, a realization that pierced her heart like a jagged shard of glass. The daunting task of survival was now entirely on her fragile shoulders.

Awakening amidst the undergrowth of the jungle, Juliane evaluated her injuries: a broken collarbone, gashes on her shoulder and calf, and a presumed concussion that left her disoriented. Juliane's sight, hindered without her glasses, made navigation arduous. Drawing on her parents' lessons, she identified familiar sounds of wildlife, helping her orient herself within the familiar, yet now fearsome, environment of the jungle.

She remained committed to finding her mother, and driven by this quest, she overcame her injuries and mustered the strength to get up, seeking solace in a packet of lollypops that had fallen from the plane.

As Juliane ventured into the heart of the Amazon, her survival instincts guided her steps. Her parents' teachings about recognizing sounds, the dangers of unfamiliar fruits, and strategies to evade piranhas came back to her. Despite her weakening state and the perpetual rain that soaked her to the core, Juliane pushed on.

A chilling encounter with the sight of dead passengers reminded her of the grim reality of her situation. Recognizing the victims' toes weren't her mother's, she felt relief before being overcome with a sense of abandonment, as she was unable to signal her presence to the distant hum of rescue planes.

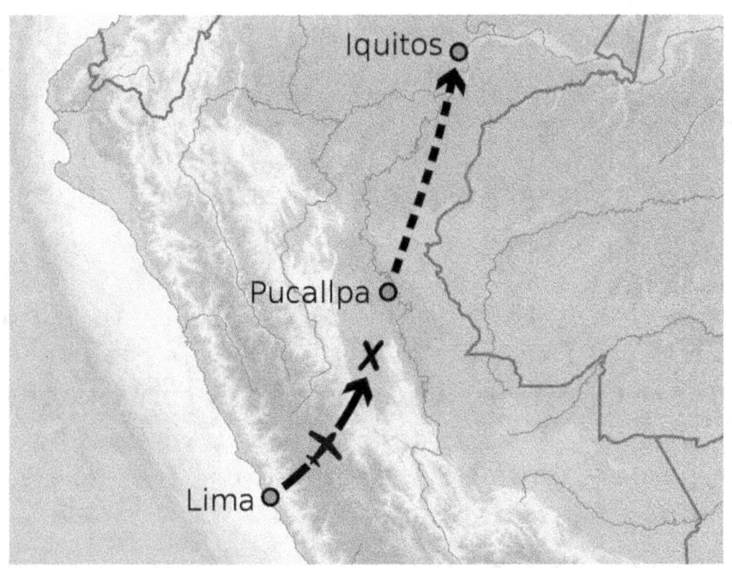

The flight path and where the plane crashed

On the tenth day of her trek, when despair had almost consumed her, Juliane stumbled upon a small hut along a stream that promised sanctuary. Inside, she found a can of petrol, which she used to sterilize the maggot-infested wound on her shoulder, echoing a treatment her father had used on a family pet.

The next day, the sound of voices drew her out of her hiding place. Peruvian fishermen, initially scared of the disheveled girl, rescued Juliane, mistaking her for a water goddess from local folklore. Exhausted, injured, yet tenaciously clinging to life, Juliane's survival story ended on a note of hope, underscoring her indomitable will and the invaluable teachings of her parents.

Over these eleven days, Juliane's grit, survival instincts, and childhood teachings of her parents helped her find her way to safety. Her parents, renowned ecologists, had moved to the Peruvian rainforest for field studies when she was fourteen.

It was there they had taught her about the delicate, intricate workings of the rainforest, lessons which later became her survival manual. "Find moving water and follow its course to a river, where human settlements are likely to be," they told her.

Four year old Juliane with her mother Maria Koepcke who was seated with her in the plane.

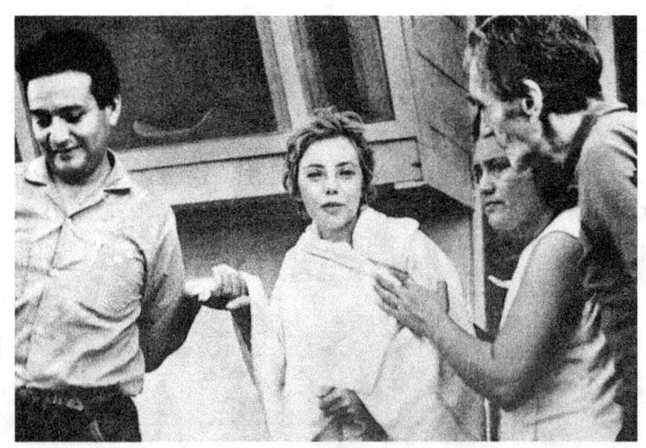

Juliane as she was brought back to
civilization by Peruvian fisherman

From Survivor to Scholar

Juliane's journey didn't end with her rescue.
After her recovery, she returned to Germany,
where she studied biology, inspired by her
parents' love for nature. Her studies eventually
led to a doctorate in mammalogy, with a
particular focus on bats.

She documented 52 species of bats at the
Panguana reserve, leading to a deep
understanding of the region's diverse wildlife,
further uncovering the secrets of the rainforest
she once braved as a teenager.

Perseverance Born of Her
Father's Resilience

Juliane's remarkable tenacity can be attributed
to her father, Hans-Wilhelm Koepcke, a single-
minded ecologist, who faced his own series of
obstacles before reaching his job in Lima.

His journey from Germany to Peru was marked by mountain treks, imprisonment in an Italian camp, and stowing away on a ship. Juliane inherited his tenacity and perseverance, traits that proved vital in her survival and later, her scholarly pursuits.

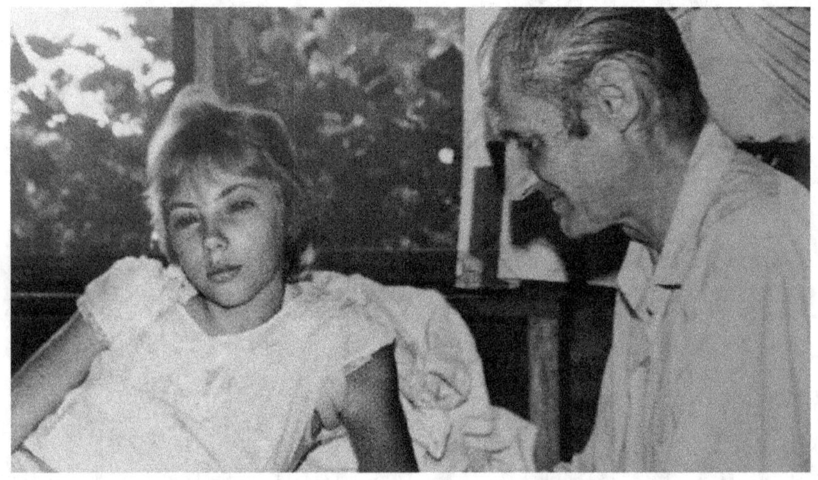

Juliane being at a hospital in Peru with her father after surviving 11 days in the Jungle

A Guardian of the Rainforest

Juliane, now Dr. Juliane Diller, has since dedicated herself to preserving the rainforest she owes her life to. As director of the Panguana Ecological Research Station, she has faced a never-ending battle against industrial and agricultural threats, climate change, and rapid deforestation. As much as 17 percent of Amazonia has already been lost, and the rise in the average temperature at Panguana by 4 degrees Celsius in the past 30 years threatens to tip the balance further.

She warns that after 20 percent deforestation, the rainforest may not recover, leading to a potential "major forest dieback and a rather sudden evolution to something else, probably a degraded savanna". This potential catastrophe has made her preservation work even more critical.

Building Bridges with the Indigenous

Recognizing that conservation efforts would only succeed with local involvement, Dr. Diller has made significant strides in establishing strong relationships with neighboring Indigenous communities. She ensures that the locals are integrated into various preservation projects, providing employment, funding schoolhouses, and raising awareness about the long-term effects of human activities on biodiversity and climate change.

"The key is getting the surrounding population to commit to preserving and protecting its environment," Dr. Diller emphasized. "Species and climate protection will only work if the locals are integrated into the projects, have a benefit for their already modest living conditions and the cooperation is transparent."

Juliane Diller working int he field photographing a venomous Viper

A Legacy OF Resilience and Hope

Fifty years since her traumatic journey through the Amazon, Dr. Diller's life is a testament to resilience and survival. She has dedicated herself to preserving the very rainforest that once put her survival to the test. Her story, one of hope and survival against the odds, serves as an inspiration for many.

"Just to have helped people and to have done something for nature means it was good that I was allowed to survive," she said, her face illuminating with a rare smile. "And for that, I am so grateful."

Today, her life is not only a tale of extraordinary survival but also an ongoing journey of steadfast dedication to protecting the fragile beauty of the rainforest. As she plans to return to Panguana when international air travel permits, it's clear that her remarkable journey, like the river that once guided her to safety, still flows on.

Dr. Juliane Diller and her husband in 2015

THE UNDERGROUND CITY THAT HOUSED 20,000

Imagine a regular day in 1963. In the heart of Turkey, a man is renovating his home in the Nevşehir Province. Suddenly, he knocks down a wall and stumbles upon a room — a mysterious, ancient room. He decides to dig further, unearthing an intricate network of tunnels leading to multiple cave-like chambers. What he discovered was not just a room, but the entrance to an entire city buried beneath the surface — the city of Derinkuyu.

Deep Down in Derinkuyu

This was no ordinary city. Derinkuyu, one of dozens of underground cities in the Cappadocia region of central Anatolia, Turkey, is a labyrinthine world of human ingenuity. It houses an elaborate network of ventilation shafts, wells, and passageways. With eight floors that plunge to a depth of 280 feet, it's the deepest of its kind.

The city was far from just a network of tunnels. It had everything a vibrant society would need — churches, food stores, livestock stalls, wine cellars, and schools. It was a fully-functioning city where life thrived underground, sheltered from the world above.

An illustration of the subterranean city found by accident.

The Marvels of Cappadocia

To truly appreciate the engineering marvel that is Derinkuyu, one must understand the unique geological history of Cappadocia. A region rich in volcanic history, Cappadocia sits on a plateau approximately 3,300 feet tall, filled with domes and pyramids created by layers of ash deposited millions of years ago.

This ash hardened into a soft, malleable rock — a perfect material for the ancient inhabitants to shape and form into these subterranean sanctuaries.

The Hittites: Master Tunnelers

Now, you might be wondering, who could have possibly carved out this colossal sanctuary? The credit likely goes to the Hittites, an ancient civilization that emerged in the 15th century BC.

They initially started by carving storage and food lockers into the soft rock, but soon realized they could create a more complex system of rooms and tunnels. This served a dual purpose: storage and protection against frequent Phrygian raids.

A Beacon of Byzantine Christianity

Picture a time when faith became a hazardous pursuit, when adherence to your religious beliefs was akin to playing with fire. This was the Byzantine era, a tumultuous period between 330 and 1461 CE, where the burgeoning Christian faith fell under the scrutiny of the ruling Umayyad and Abbasid dynasties. Practicing Christianity wasn't just difficult, it was dangerous.

Underground gathering room in Derinkuyu

In this precarious landscape, Derinkuyu offered a lifeline, a literal underground refuge for the devout. Tucked away beneath the earth, this subterranean city provided an opportunity to live out their faith in peace, albeit under the earth's crust rather than under the sun. For these early Christians, this choice was not just preferable, it was essential for their survival.

But Derinkuyu was more than a survivalist bunker. Within the intricate network of caves and tunnels, the Christian community thrived, carving out more than just a life for themselves. They carved out a spiritual sanctuary, sculpting churches from the rock, spaces where faith could flourish away from the prying eyes above ground. These cavernous chapels, still marked today with the symbols of their devotion, were the stages for sacred services, the sound of hymns reverberating off the stony walls.

Further, the city became a fortress of learning, fostering Christian knowledge in the safety of its hidden rooms. Young minds were nurtured here, taught to read and write, introduced to the pillars of their faith amidst the quiet strength of the rocks around them. Derinkuyu was more than a refuge; it was a beacon of hope, allowing a beleaguered community to preserve their culture and religion even as tensions simmered above ground.

An interior view from a church in the Göreme
Open Air Museum, Cappadocia, central Turkey

Today, the remnants of Derinkuyu whisper tales of a resolute past, of a community that held onto its faith even under immense pressure. As one traverses its silent corridors, the echo of ancient prayers may be long gone, but the spirit of resilience and religious dedication persists. In the face of adversity, the early Christians of Derinkuyu didn't just survive; they demonstrated the enduring power of faith, undeterred even when compelled to take it underground.

Carved out of the rocks, these passages was a full city underground.

Beyond Survival: Life Underground

But the underground city was more than just a sanctuary — it was home. During times of peace, the caves served as cold storage facilities and livestock barns. In times of peril, the residents carried on their lives as usual — commerce thrived with communal meeting areas, dining rooms, grocers, even shopping spaces. The city was equipped with an underground river, wells for drinking water, and thousands of ventilation shafts to ensure a healthy living environment.

Derinkuyu Today: A Glimpse into the Past

Today, Derinkuyu serves as a historical testament to human adaptability. A mere 10% of the city is open to the public, but even that fraction allows visitors to marvel at this subterranean wonder. Each narrow passageway, each concealed entrance, each blackened tunnel echoes stories of a thriving society that once existed beneath the surface.

Derinkuyu reminds us of a time when communities had to burrow deep into the earth, transforming a network of tunnels into a city teeming with life. A time when, against all odds, 20,000 people found a way to thrive — deep down under.

Early morning hours in Göreme, when 100s of
hot air balloons take to the sky.
It's a beautiful sight to see.

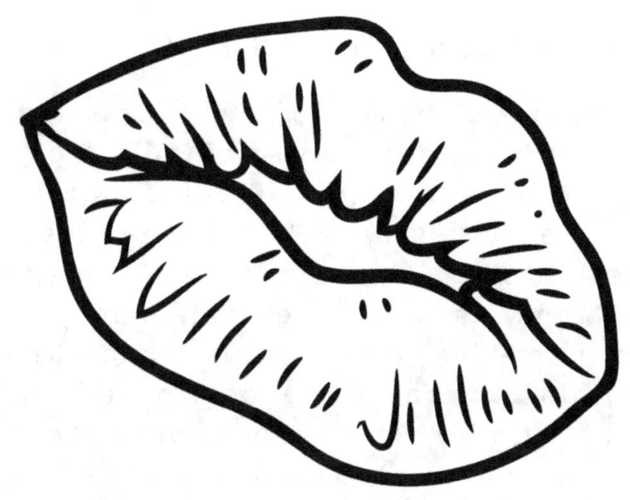

THE STORY BEHIND THE FAMOUS KISS

August 15, 1945, marked a pivotal moment in history. The streets of New York City, especially Times Square, were teeming with joy as news of Japan's surrender echoed through every corner. World War II was finally over. Amidst the elated cheers and relieved sighs, a singular moment of euphoria was captured that would go on to symbolize an era of peace following years of strife - a sailor in a passionate embrace with a woman in a nurse's uniform. Renowned photographer Alfred Eisenstaedt immortalized this spontaneous kiss, making it an iconic testament of the time.

The Mystery Unraveled

For years, the identities of the couple locked in the impromptu embrace remained shrouded in mystery. Who were the jubilant sailor and the woman who found herself in his arms? Their identities would eventually be unveiled as George Mendonsa and Greta Zimmer Friedman. But the narrative behind this candid moment was neither one of romance nor a contrived photo opportunity. The story behind the famous kiss was as unscripted and unforeseen as the moment itself. Newer facial recognition technology was used to get confirmation that the pair in the photo are Mendonsa and Friedman.

The Famous Kiss at Time Square, August 15, 1945

The Unexpected Burst of Jubilation

On that day, Greta Zimmer Friedman was working as a dental assistant. The fervor of the celebrations pulled her outside, eager to be part of the historic moment. Amidst the exuberant crowd, George Mendonsa, a sailor overflowing with joy, spotted her. He had just heard the news while on a date with Rita Petrie at Radio City Music Hall and was overcome by a wave of relief and gratitude. Seeing Friedman in her uniform, he was reminded of the nurses who had cared for his injured comrades during the war.

Acting on impulse, Mendonsa said, "The excitement of the war being over, plus I had a few drinks. So when I saw the nurse, I grabbed her and I kissed her." This spontaneous action, fuelled by a mix of elation and gratitude, resulted in one of the most enduring images of the 20th century. Friedman later recounted the unexpected moment, "He was just holding me tight. I'm not sure about the kiss… it was just somebody celebrating. It wasn't a romantic event."

Rita Petrie, who was his date that day said later in an interview with CBS "Either I was dopey or something, but it didn't bother me!" She is seen in the background of the photo. Petrie ended up being Mendonsa's wife of 70 years.

Time Square celebrations on V-J Day

Alfred Eisenstaedt: Capturing History

Behind every great photograph is an equally compelling photographer. In this case, it was Alfred Eisenstaedt, an American photojournalist of German origin, who happened to be in Times Square that day. Working for Life Magazine, he was tasked with capturing the celebration of the end of the war. He discovered the perfect moment at 5:51 pm.

Alfred Eisenstaedt with his camera that
took the famous photo

"I saw a sailor running along the street grabbing any and every girl in sight...Then suddenly, in a flash, I saw something white being grabbed. I turned around and clicked the moment the sailor kissed the nurse," Eisenstaedt recalled. His quick action and sharp eye resulted in a photograph that would adorn the cover of Life Magazine and become his most renowned image.

Eisenstaedt described a portion of his success as luck, but also emphasized the importance of vigilance. He carried a small Leica IIIa camera, which made him less noticeable. He felt this contributed to the authenticity of his shots. "They don't take me too seriously with my little camera. I don't come as a photographer. I come as a friend," he once said.

After The Kiss

Following the spontaneous kiss, Mendonsa and Friedman went about their own ways. Their identities remained a mystery for years until the 1980s, when Life Magazine and Eisenstaedt contacted them for a reunion to commemorate and recreate the iconic moment.

George Mendonsa with his photo with Friedman, Middletown, Rhode Island in 2009.

Controversy Amid Celebration

Though widely celebrated as an emblem of joy, the photograph has been the center of controversy in recent years. Critics have called out the non-consensual nature of the kiss.

Friedman herself acknowledged this, saying, "I felt he was very strong, he was just holding me tight, and I'm not sure I — about the kiss because, you know, it was just somebody really celebrating.

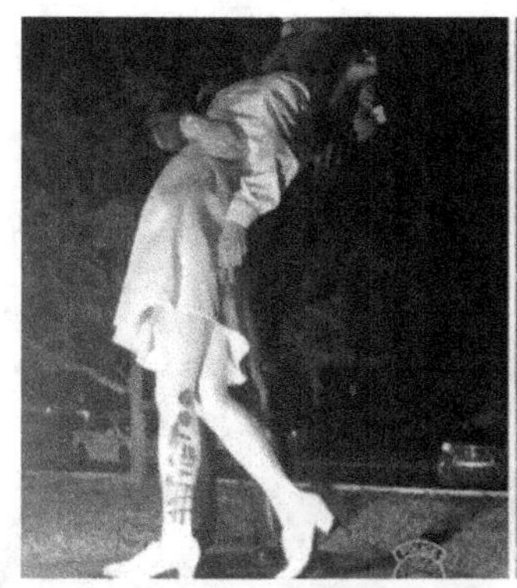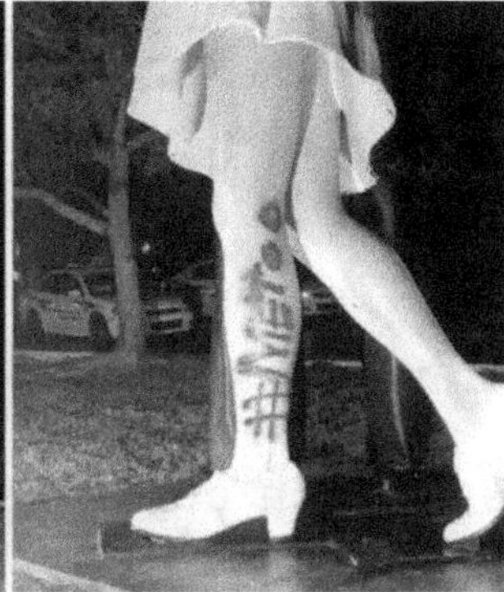

The kissing sailor picture has come under scrutiny more recently, with many accusing the Mendonsa of assault. Photograph: Sarasota Police Department

But it wasn't a romantic event. It was just an event of thank God the war is over kind of thing," adding "It wasn't my choice to be kissed. The guy just came over and kissed or grabbed me."

Mendonsa was not alone in his enthusiastic celebration that day. Other sailors, overwhelmed by the relief of the war's end, were also kissing women in Times Square. Friedman recalled, "They were happy they didn't have to go back to war. They had had enough. So, you know, they were not the only sailor that kissed women."

More people celebrating V-J Day, Aug 14, 1945

An Enduring Legacy

Although both Friedman and Mendonsa have passed away, their legacy lives on through the photograph. A statue in Florida immortalizes their famous kiss, ensuring that their spontaneous moment of joy and relief endures. The photograph continues to be one of the most iconic images of the 20th century. It's more than just a captured moment of passion; it's a symbol of humanity's collective sigh of relief at the end of a war-torn era, reminding us of the joyous, impromptu moments that can become the stories of a lifetime.

THE MOST EXPENSIVE PAINTING EVER SOLD

In November 2017, the art world was stunned when an enigmatic painting of Christ called Salvator Mundi sold for a record-shattering $450 million at auction. But the painting's backstory is equally fascinating - from its disputed origins and miraculous rediscovery to the intrigue surrounding its disappearance after the sale. This is the story of the world's most expensive painting and the mystery that still surrounds it.

The Rarity of a da Vinci

Part of what drove Salvator Mundi's astronomical price is the rarity of a Leonardo da Vinci painting. Da Vinci's oeuvre only contains around 20 surviving paintings, since he was more renowned in his day as a sculptor, scientist and inventor. That scarcity imbues his paintings with a magical aura amongst art collectors and historians.

Fully restored Salvator Mundi by Leonardo da Vinci

The prospect of a previously undiscovered da Vinci painting emerging is the art world equivalent of discovering buried treasure. It captures the imagination with the possibility that more of Da Vinci's genius may still be out there, lost or misattributed.

This sense of profound discovery is part of what created the speculative frenzy around Salvator Mundi when it was re-identified as an authentic da Vinci.

The Painting's Origins

Salvator Mundi, Latin for "Savior of the World", depicts a haloed Christ in Renaissance-era robes making a blessing gesture with one hand while holding a crystal orb. Da Vinci is thought to have painted it in the early 1500s, possibly for King Louis XII of France. The composition was known from da Vinci's sketches.

But the painting disappeared from historical records after the 18th century. In the 1900s, it bizarrely resurfaced in an estate sale marketed as a copy before again vanishing. Forgotten in a Baton Rouge home, it was eventually auctioned in 2005 for just $1,175 to a consortium of art dealers who saw glimmers of authenticity beneath the painting's poor condition.

Salvator Mundi Pre-Restoration

An Extensive Restoration

The dealers brought Salvator Mundi to renowned conservator Dianne Modestini for restoration. Under layers of botched overpainting, she uncovered passages resembling Da Vinci's style - including the blessing hand perfectly preserved. Further forensic study revealed pentimenti, or changes to the composition, suggesting an original work rather than a copy.

The dramatic restoration finally convinced authorities this was da Vinci's long-lost Salvator Mundi. The discovery made global headlines given the painting's rich but obscure provenance and its miraculous rebirth through conservation. It was like finding a precious relic thought to have been lost forever.

Painting restorer Dianne Modestini in a scene from The Lost Leonardo.

Record-Breaking Sale and Disappearance

In 2013, Salvator Mundi was purchased privately for $127 million by Swiss art dealer Yves Bouvier on behalf of Russian billionaire Dmitry Rybolovlev. But its public debut came in 2017 when Rybolovlev sold it through Christie's auction house in New York. Auctioneer Jussi Pilkkanen opened bidding at $100 million as spectators waited breathlessly. The bidding climbed steadily until the hammer dropped at a jaw-dropping $450 million, obliterating the previous record for a painting sold at auction.

Yet the anonymous buyer, later revealed as a Saudi prince acting on behalf of Mohammed bin Salman, has never displayed the painting publicly. After being slated to appear at the Louvre Abu Dhabi, its unveiling was mysteriously postponed indefinitely. The painting's location remains unknown, prompting speculation about whether its new Saudi owners have doubts about its authenticity.

The painting's staggering sale price and disappearance from view have only added to its mystique. The public is left wondering whether Salvator Mundi is a rightful Da Vinci or simply an over-restored imitation. Its whereabouts continue to be one of the art world's biggest mysteries.

Detail of the globe in Salvator Mundi.
(Credit: Louvre Abu Dhabi / Wikipedia)

Leonardo da Vinci's Allure

Regardless of unresolved debates about Salvator Mundi's authenticity, its sale illustrates the unique allure of a da Vinci painting. The possibility of it being an original was enough to drive the highest auction price ever paid for artwork.

Salvator Mundi on display at Christie's salesroom in London in 2017, ahead of its sale for $450 million.

Da Vinci's renown derives not only from his art but his extraordinary intellect. The term "Renaissance Man" originates from da Vinci's diverse talents. Beyond painting, he studied anatomy, botany, geology, designed machines, and made breakthroughs in fields from optics to hydraulics.

The Mona Lisa by Leonardo da Vinci.
The most famous painting in the world.

His most famous work, the Mona Lisa, has become synonymous with art itself. The Louvre, where it hangs, is the world's most-visited museum. For collectors and institutions, a da Vinci represents the pinnacle of artistic genius. The potential discovery of a lost painting creates once-in-a-lifetime opportunities, along with intense competition and speculation.

Salvator Mundi's amazing path from flea market discard to most expensive artwork ever symbolizes da Vinci's unmatched cultural legacy. The painting's ambiguous fate is a testament to the mysteries still surrounding Da Vinci's life that tantalize art lovers today. For those dreaming of finding a Da Vinci in an attic or storage unit, it shows such a windfall may be more complicated than imagined.

OPERATION VEGETARIAN

As World War II ravaged Europe in the early 1940s, both sides sought any advantage that could turn the tide of the conflict. Great Britain hatched one of the most sinister secret plans of the war - Operation Vegetarian - a biological attack to cripple Germany's food supply using anthrax-infected cattle cakes. Though never carried out, the chilling plan revealed the desperation of nations and moral compromises made in wartime.

World War II had expanded into a grueling global conflict by 1942. Nazi Germany's occupation stretched across much of Europe after blitzkrieg victories against Poland, France, and other nations. The British Isles stood nearly alone against Hitler's march across the continent. As the Nazis considered biological weapons, Prime Minister Winston Churchill resolved that "we should concentrate our attention upon B.W. [biological warfare], with a view to putting ourselves in a position to use it should the need arise." Thus began the British mission to develop its own biological arsenal.

Sir Winston Churchill

The Search for a Secret Weapon

A top-secret team was assembled in 1942 at Porton Down, the British chemical and biological weapons research center in southwest England. Their task? Find a way to retaliate if Hitler resorted to germ warfare against the United Kingdom. After weighing options ranging from botulinum toxin to typhoid, the government settled on developing a strain of anthrax.

Anthrax is caused by spore-forming Bacillus anthracis bacteria that occur naturally in soils. Grazing animals ingest the resilient spores which multiply and produce lethal toxins once inside a host. With a fatality rate around 75% in humans, anthrax could decimate populations if intentionally spread. But how to deliver a potential attack?

After acquiring a highly virulent anthrax strain known as Vollum, Porton Down scientists proposed dropping anthrax-laced cattle cakes from aircraft over Germany. The cakes would be eaten by cattle that would succumb to anthrax. Their infected meat would then enter the German food supply, triggering mass casualties when consumed by people.

Beyond physical harm, the British theorized that such an attack could create crippling uncertainty and fear around eating meat, lowering German morale.

The mission even earned a darkly ironic nickname - Operation Vegetarian. Field tests soon commenced to turn concept into deadly reality.

Testing Anthrax on British Sheep

To validate their anthrax cattle cakes, Porton Down needed to conduct live field trials - but where? In 1942, the desolate, privately-owned island of Gruinard off the Scottish coast was chosen for its remoteness. If anthrax contamination occurred, the secluded island could be quarantined with minimal risk to populated areas.

In July 1942, Royal Air Force bombers flew over Gruinard and dropped anthrax-filled bombs across a flock of sheep. Over the next few days, all 60 sheep perished from inhaling anthrax spores that suffocated their lungs. The tests were deemed a success - anthrax could be dispersed over a large area and cause rapid death. But consequences would soon emerge that threatened the mainland.

Collateral Damage from Anthrax Tests

After the Gruinard field test, the anthrax bacteria permeated the island's soil, persisting for decades. A storm later unearthed infected sheep carcasses that washed ashore on the Scottish mainland just 1km away. Local dogs scavenged the carcasses, contracting anthrax and triggering an outbreak in mainland livestock.

Over 100 animals died before authorities controlled the spread, underscoring the indiscriminate nature of biological weapons. Meanwhile, Porton Down forged ahead mass-producing 5 million anthrax-injected linseed cattle cakes by 1943 - enough to blanket fields across Germany. But by early 1944, Germany's defeat seemed imminent and Operation Vegetarian was abandoned. Yet disposal of unused anthrax proved as vexing as its development.

Gruiard Island also now dubbed 'Anthrax Island'.
Photo taken in 1986 (via The Scotsman)

Disposing of Unused Anthrax Cakes

With Operation Vegetarian scrapped by war's end, British authorities faced an anthrax cleanup dilemma - how to safely destroy millions of anthrax-filled cattle cakes? All but two crates of the lethal treats were ultimately incinerated under military supervision. But the threat of any cakes escaping still concerned officials given the viability of anthrax spores for decades if buried.

The most pressing issue remained decontaminating Gruinard Island after rendering it dangerously inhospitable from the tests. Initially kept under quarantine, major decontamination efforts began in 1986 using seawater and fogging with formaldehyde. It took 4 years and over $7 million before Gruinard was finally declared anthrax-free and sold back to original owners in 1990, almost 50 years after first use.

The drastic measures underscored the sobering power of biological agents against exposed populations. While much of developed Scotland recovered, the Gruinard anthrax trials left permanent scars on an unassuming island. Would a full-scale attack on Germany have scarred its people and lands just as profoundly?

Could it have worked?

On paper, Operation Vegetarian appeared a ruthless blow against civilian populations under Nazi occupation in Europe. But biological weapons rarely follow predictable scripts. Could the cattle cake plan have significantly hindered Germany's war machine if enacted?

While ingesting anthrax-tainted meat likely would have proved fatal for thousands, resulting food shortages may have been replaceable through rationing programs. Germany's massive territory could also dilute anthrax's spread compared to Gruinard's concentrated doses. Eliminating traces of anthrax across vast lands to restore agriculture could have taken years, however.

There were also moral arguments against replicating Operation Vegetarian. Anthrax killed indiscriminately, afflicting rural farmers and urban families alike, Axis and Allied citizens across borders. Some military leaders expressed concerns about provoking Hitler to retaliate with his own biological attacks in a dangerous escalation.

Ultimately, the plan remained theoretical. Hitler never approved germ warfare during World War II, likely avoiding retaliation in kind. But Britain's willingness to develop such weapons underscored the temptations that even open societies face during existential wars.

The Allure of Biological Weapons

What made political leaders sanction programs like Operation Vegetarian against entire civilian populations? Biological weapons have always held morbid allure for militaries seeking an asymmetric advantage, yet are banned by modern treaties.

On one hand, collapsing enemy food supplies could turn occupied civilians against their leaders to sue for peace, military strategists argued. Populations weakened by hunger were also more prone to succumbing to deadly bacteria. After withstanding years of German bombardment, some British officials likely wanted revenge through any available means too.

German bombers raid London in September, 1940.
The bombing continued until May, 1941

Yet these rationales violated codes protecting noncombatants. They also risked propelling an endless biological arms race of retaliation. Once Pandora's box was opened, neither side could turn back.

Fortunately, Hitler never embraced germ warfare, for reasons still unclear. But it was less an act of conscience than pragmatism. Germany zealously developed chemical weapons and delivery systems that could have been converted to biological agents if Hitler wished. Perceived mental and physical weaknesses after nearly dying from poison gas in WWI may have personally disgusted him to biological weapons though.

Nonetheless, Nazi officials dabbled in entomological warfare research, breeding disease-carrying insects. Had Hitler ordered its use, a special SS unit under Kurt Blome was tasked with waging biological warfare. While Operation Vegetarian idled, the potential ingredients for apocalypse remained at hand for both sides.

Anthrax at Porton Down

While Operation Vegetarian never materialized, Britain's investment in anthrax research cast a long shadow. Fearing Soviet biological attacks, the UK accelerated development of anthrax alongside smallpox, botulinum and other agents through the 1950s before finally renouncing biological weapons in 1956.

The Soviets, Japanese, Americans and others, however, pressed onwards with disturbing biological programs during the Cold War, necessitating vigilance and preparedness. Research at facilities like Porton Down shifted focus to countermeasure development and defense — dual-use work continues to spark controversy today.

Government scientists from Porton Down conducting decontamination works from 1986.

The compound at Porton Down remains one of the world's premier government laboratories specializing in chemicals, vaccines, pharmaceuticals, and pathogen identification. During the 2018 Novichok poisoning of former Russian spy Sergei Skripal, nearby public health experts rushed samples to Porton Down for analysis within hours, tracing the nerve agent back to Russia.

Reflecting on Operation Vegetarian's Legacy

The organization is also partnering with Oxford University in testing vaccines against COVID-19. While Porton Down maintains it is "one of the most scrutinized organizations in the world," its genesis in programs like Operation Vegetarian still fuels unease about the ethics of its mission. The allure of weaponizing biology, so tempting in wartime, has never fully faded.

Reflecting on Operation Vegetarian's Legacy
As WWII entered its final, desperate years, governments faced difficult choices and ethical tradeoffs. Operation Vegetarian exemplified the cold calculations made when societies feel threatened to the core. Though it was never enacted, the program revealed what humanity is capable of under existential duress.

Yet biological weapons also demonstrate that science without conscience threatens our shared bonds and moral codes in wartime and peace. Thankfully, Operation Vegetarian was abandoned as an immoral means to victory over fascism. Its legacy should remind us of the dangers whenever nations view human lives as mere statistics and instruments of war.

Though Allied nations embraced moral compromises against totalitarian enemies, these acts did not ultimately define their character. As Churchill himself reflected on England's darkest moments, "The nation had the lion's heart even if at times it did not have the lion's strength." May we retain our humanity, lest we become the monsters we fight.

Hello Reader!

As we close the pages of this collection of remarkable true stories, from a bouncer that became a Pope to Einstein's stolen brain, we're reminded of the incredible depth and breadth of the human experience. Fact is often much more fascinating than fiction.

Human stories such as the ones contained in this book have the power to inspire, educate, and transform. They encourage us to look closer at the world around us, to ask questions, and to seek out the remarkable stories hiding in plain sight.

This is why I wrote this book and it is why I run the website **FactBrainiac.com.** You can find many more stories on our website.

If you enjoyed these stories, visit our website, and sign up for free newsletter where we share mind bending stories on a weekly basis.

I thank you from the bottom of my heart for purchasing this book and I hope to see you in your inbox!

Warmest regards,

Billy @ FactBrainiac.com